Beyond Every Wall

Becoming the 1st Black, Female Transplant Surgeon

Velma P. Scantlebury, M.D.

Beyond Every Wall

Becoming the 1st, Black, Female Kidney Transplant Surgeon

by Velma P. Scantlebury, M.D.

ISBN: 978-0-578-40554-4

Permissions for use of any part of this book may be requested, or book purchase orders may be placed by contacting:

V P Scantlebury, M.D. Attention Orders, or Attention Permissions

Inquiries@BeyondEveryWall.com Newark DE US

1. Non-Fiction

Sole Author & Publisher: V P Scantlebury, M.D.

www.BeyondEveryWall.com

Front Cover Photo Credit/Copyright: Jaryd Niles-Morris

Cover Design: 2Rise Publishing
Interior Design: 2Rise, Publishing
Editor: James Leland Randall

For my parents, Kathleen and Delacey Scantlebury

For my husband, Dr. Harvey White

For my biological children, Akela and Aisha,
as well as Noela, Ala, Adeola and Mary

For the good doctors whose examples continue to guide me.

The Journey

OPERATION

"Where the heck did you get your medical training? Did you do a correspondence course?"

He was in command, demanding our attention, and my attention. I was sweating, scared, annoyed, and offended.

The operating theatre could be just that; a theatre.

It was time to remove the damaged liver. The patient was a six-year-old girl. There was a history of congenital liver disease with three previous operations that failed to correct the problem. The liver needed to be replaced with a new one.

Dr. Starzl unabashedly continued his tirade. He was before an audience, and an operation was his element.

The lights were so bright that they were as much blue haze as the means to a shadowless environment. Beyond the lights stood a number of visiting doctors and professors; each was silently going over how they would do better than those of us working under the lights, and under a demanding master surgeon. It was a day, and place, that a young transplant surgeon wanted, and dreaded.

There was scarred tissue everywhere. The edges of the old liver were adherent to the other organs in the abdomen. The fingers of his left hand seemed to glide into the spaces that needed attention. They created openings using his special "Starzl" scissors to release the tissues. The edges were thinner and more rounded than standard surgical scissors. As his hand released itself from those dark places, it was followed by stream of blood.

Quickly suctioning the red liquid, the area was irrigated with saline, allowing the organ structures to be visible again. The tension in the room was palpable.

Observing the beads of perspiration accumulating on his forehead, the circulating nurse worked her way through the crowd to wipe the sweat before the drops could land below.

Somewhere beyond my focus, Dr. Starzl was still in the midst of his comments about our shortcomings. He continued to fire the insults, berating me for breaking the 7-0 suture. He had asked me to tie it around an unreasonably thin piece of nondescript tissue. It was on the right side of the abdomen. I was on the left, with only one shoulder squeezed between the drapes, between the two other assistants, and across the tiny body of our patient.

The child's breathing was paced by the breathing machine; the heart rate was rapid even for a child unaware of all the actions in and around her body. Each beat of the heart was echoed by a competing gasp from the loud anesthetic machine.

The child's face was smooth, relaxed, and peaceful. Perhaps, it was the only peaceful expression in the room.

The lights were still blue, hot and bright. The air was kept warm, so that the patient's body would not cool unnecessarily. We were all still intimidated by the skill, and the demeanor, of Dr. Starzl. My hands began to cramp.

A child's life was at stake here; not just egos, and feelings, and imagined illustrious careers and glories. I needed to stay focused on the case, in spite of the pressure that comes with working with a renowned surgeon.

Dr. Starzl did not allow music in his operating rooms. We only had the sighs of his exasperation with us and the occasional rise of a voice from an operating room circulating nurse: each counting to keep track of the bloody sponges passed off by the scrub nurse. Ten new ones passed up by the scrub nurse. Ten soaked ones removed to the bucket below.

There is a smell to old blood. To us, those under the lights, it could barely be detected. For me, the smell was my own breath against the mask; it was my ambition, my fear, and my understanding that the entire life of this tiny patient depended upon our success. It was all wet, and profound.

The forty-pound child's heart beat steadily, one hundred times per minute. Dr. Starzl's demand was for near silence.

"Please, hold the breath! Can you slow down the heartbeat? I need to work, here!"

The demands were, first, about controlling the patient. They were applicable to us, to me. I needed to hold my breath, to control, to slow my heart-rate - all to survive.

I adjusted my right hip to ease the pain of standing for so long at odd angles and in fear of my mentor and the consequences of any possible mistake. My hands were still cramping. He was still unhappy. The patient was in another world. The audience was silent.

My next task was to place my right hand up in the upper, left area of the abdomen. It would serve to hold back some of the structures there. In a pediatric surgery there is not much space. My job, in this case, could have been done easily, using a metal retractor. That was not allowed. Dr. Starzl was having more fun humiliating me, and the other first-year fellow, to allow that simple, luxurious, deference to available technology.

There was perspiration, sweat; it was mine. Somewhere, a controlling part of my mind allowed a small amount of time to luxuriate in how I got there.

I had just completed my chief residency year in general surgery. I was an incredible surgeon. I knew this. That mantra was a silent chant, inside my mind, between my own heartbeats. The hours of surgery on the child bore on.

I thought, "I deserve better than this."

I thought, "I will not let him break me."

Some part of me, some voice inside, convinced me - for these hours - that I could drown out the master surgeon's taunts.

I was an "apprentice." And, this is how we were treated. It was how we were expected to learn and remember. I remember.

I started listening to a tune, just in my head. I didn't get much beyond the first verse.

Dr. Starzl was yelling again. Yelling in a small room with a bright, bluish light, an audience in shadow, a cadre of nurses and technicians, three annoyed, awed, fearful pediatric transplant surgery fellows, and a child, not just a child's body, open before us. He was yelling! Still.

"Are you listening to anything I am saying?"

"Yes. Yes, sir. I am."

Dr. Brandon, a second-year fellow, shifted from leg to leg as he braced for the next round of insults. The liver had to be removed exactly, precisely; it had to be only as Dr. Starzl directed, was famous for, and demanded.

Dr. Starzl made it look effortless. Why else would we endure his loud disapproval? We wanted to be that good ... perhaps more kind; but, just that good.

CLOSING

Each hour that passed seemed like three. My sweat was from fear and tension; the air was still cold, to us above the table. Only the patient's inner, physical works were bright, without shadow. In my mind, I knew that all smelled clean, clinical, void of anything except a constant heartbeat on a stainless steel table and the full attention of a score of people looking to learn how miracles are made.

Once the old liver was removed, Dr. Starzl flew out of the room and left Dr. Brandon to "clean up" according to Starzl-specific instructions. We could all now exhale, drop our shoulders, and emit sighs of our own.

The child's breath remained shallow, steady; she remained, unaware.

The new liver was being prepared on a back table in a darker part of the room, a part beyond our current focus.

Dr. Carlos was a junior attending physician in pediatric transplant surgery. We welcomed his calm and soothing demeanor. What seemed like days were only an intense two hours with Dr. Starzl. That time was gone. We were left to ready the patient for the next phase of the surgery: implanting the new liver. The pale brown structure was brought to the field. Shiny and smooth, it glistened under the bright lights, as it was placed in its new home. It fitted perfectly in the space left behind from the old liver.

The calm in the room was new, and refreshing. Dr. Carlos made his movements smooth and deft as he worked through the vessel connections. We were ready for the unclamping and the release of blood into the new liver.

The anesthesiologist was warned to watch for detrimental blood pressure issues, or if we alerted that there was excessive bleeding.

Somewhere there were echoes of Dr. Starzl's bluster and of his precision and demands. Excellence was still demanded, and expected. We all relished, and absorbed, the new, quieter, way to achieve it.

The new liver was fed blood and its pale brown color changed to reddish brown. Things were going to be okay. The change was a beautiful, and miraculous, sight.

As the donated liver seemed to awaken in the child's body, we watched. The lap pads were removed, and the bleeding resolved.

The liver started to do one of its jobs; that of producing bile. In the transplant community bile is called liquid gold. Yes. Things were going to be okay.

It is funny how a word can mean so many things. We rejoiced as the child's new liver began producing bile. Yet, the word bile is often reviled and associated with pain and anger; but not in this situation. It was a symbol of success: the reassurance that the liver was working well.

I found myself smiling beneath my mask. The child was going to be alright. I had survived an operation with the great Dr. Starzl. And, I had done it all after starting in a place where success was not guaranteed. More important, the child survived us all.

We left the operating room and faced cooler lights and rest.

PHENOMENAL WOMAN

Definitely, my mother, was the first phenomenal woman I ever knew.

She married at age sixteen. By the age of thirty she had given birth to seven children.

Whatever I have done, and whatever I might do, will always be pale in comparison to what I see as her accomplishments.

My mother lacked nothing in vision and determination. She had an innate understanding of how to make things better for her family; and, she had a plan to make sure those better things happened.

She was a serious woman.

Living in a time when schooling was completed by age sixteen, contributing to the workforce was the expected next step. My mother, instead, switched from childhood to motherhood. She desired a large family, much unlike her own, having only one sister.

My mother recognized the power that education allowed one to wield. She made sure that all of her children understood not only the value of education, but that acquiring a great education was not an option. It was a necessity, an expectation, a demand to be made for self and for family.

Barbados, our home, was a British colony until the late 1960s. Great Britain was the "mother country", even though we did not look British or were we treated as full British citizens in everyday interactions. The single good thing about the state of our country's relationship with the British Isles was access to a British education. As a child, one had little choice in schooling: the demand was, be present. On a small island, truancy was not an option. Watchful eyes on every corner sent instant messages of one's actions before you arrived home. Even without home telephones. The consequences fell in line with 'spare the rod, spoil the child.'

My mother made sure we were always present at school. Excellence was demanded. As part of a new generation, we had better options for further education. The University of the West Indies, was founded in 1948, and it opened its campus in Barbados in 1963.

The expectation was that, beyond high school, one either went to the local university, or to England for further studies. 'Further' is the operative here.

In November 1966 Barbados was freed from being a British colony. From the near side of the Atlantic, during his brief time in office, President John F. Kennedy loosened the rules on travel visas. With those changes, if you lived in Barbados, the world became a bigger place; water or stone, there were fewer walls to scale to explore achieving success in an entire world.

My mum, true to her place in my heart as a heroine, had expectations of her own, for herself. At the age of forty she set her sights on taking herself, and the entire family, to the United States.

The opportunities for advancement, for accumulating wealth, for snaring the future she knew we all deserved were all tied to excellence in educational pursuits. That was irresistible to her, for us. It was our obligation - to her, to ourselves.

She was a serious woman.

The consensus is that I look like my mother. On several trips back to Barbados, older friends, who had not seen me in many years, or were seeing me for the first time, would remark how much I resemble my mother.

Now, I am the serious woman.

I want to resemble her in more than looks. Although, looking like she did can get other reactions.

Her internal seriousness showed in her face.

Moving from one task to another, in nearly every hospital where I have worked, there have been times when I was lost in thought. This was often a spell broken by someone admonishing me to "Smile, life is not that bad." Truly, it is not bad. And, I am not mad.

It is just this face.

On more than one occasion I have had someone say something like, "You disagree, don't you? I can see the look on your face." It is not always the case. It is just the look I inherited.

My mother's determination showed on her face. Now I wear that face and I carry the determination - proudly.

Often, I wonder what my mother would have become had she chosen a different path.

If she had become a professional educator, her classes would have been the strictest. They would also have been the most rewarding; even if the value and reward were not realized until much later.

Both in Barbados, and later in Brooklyn, my mother was our guide, and our rock.

I rarely asked what my mother was contemplating when she was in her own place, her own "lost in her thoughts." She would stand in our small kitchen, mechanically preparing the day's breadfruit and fish. I watched for a long while, as if staring at her would somehow let me see inside her head.

That day, she wore a green dress under her apron. Her hands worked quickly. They knew what to do. Her mind was, obviously, elsewhere. I imagined that she was in the midst of prayer, or most quietly humming a hymn. Perhaps she was planning the course of our lives for the years ahead.

Her jaw was set, as if she were ready for some resistance I could not see. I came to think of this as her "America look". The knife worked itself through the breadfruit, as if it remembered. The breadfruit offered no fight. Perhaps she was rehearsing.

The leap was hers to take. And she was going to take it. God had her back. Those mounting credit bills that allowed for weekly groceries would be managed in the months to come. Her payout from the neighborhood "sou-sou" would come before the end of the year. This was her "money in a jar". It was emptied twice a year, and her time would come – at just the right time.

STATELY MAN

My dad joined the police force when he was twenty-three years old, newly married to my young, and already determined, mother. They had a child - Mary, and another on the way.

It was not an easy decision to leave the security and comforts of his supporting family. But, it was time to strike out with his own family, and to acknowledge the long-term harms the unsteadiness of his previous employment would bring.

One of seven brothers, at the age of 14 he was given the role of cooking for his older working brothers. The sudden death of his mother left them with no caretaker. His own Dad had left for America 6 years before. At sixteen years of age, he started working various jobs, still having the responsibilities of home. The strike of the train system required him to walk 16 miles to some jobs.

Married for only two years, at age twenty-one, the opportunity to join the police academy was bitter-sweet, as he was away from home six days a week for six months. Ten miles each way was his walk home every Sunday to see his family.

As time progressed, and with the goodness of God, he was afforded a loan to build a home in Bridgetown. His only requirements were being close to great schools and a short walk to the ocean.

As his family grew, he made the necessary adjustments to support the new additions and new demands. Not every 'want' was fulfilled, but the needs were all met with necessary, and available provisions.

There were also fun times. As a constable, my dad was able to get us in to the Christmas celebration at the District A Police Station. We saw it as a chance to receive the only 'real' toy for the holiday. We were children and fell to thinking that only those 'store-bought' toys were real gifts. But, more, it was a celebration for policemen and their families.

As most children, we knew little of the true struggles of a parent. I only knew that though he did not show it, or say it, my father mourned lost battles fought for his children. Those battles were as small as the 'right' gift for each child, and as large as the biggest opportunities to reward our work toward the goal of academic excellence.

This is not to say that my dad lacked humor, or was a stranger to conviviality. He enjoyed a good laugh, having one and making one. When I laugh, I can hear my father.

As he wound the threads of funny tales of times past, his contagious smile always preceded a cascade of laughter - his own. Often, he would be overcome by his own humor and fold into rumbles and riffs of his own mirth before even finishing the story.

We were fortunate to have parents who always built us up. So, there was never any beratement or sarcasm directed toward us through my father's laughter. Though, I am sure that some of our antics brought him to the edge of an outright guffaw.

Stories of his encounters with the 'law-breaking' residents, visitors to the island, the weekend 'rum drinkers' brawls, along with the machete-armed jealous husbands, formed the basis for some scary and often just plain fun times. Many was the evening we sat around enjoying the end of day and the tastes that the cooking smells had promised hours earlier.

There were tales of criminals hiding out in the nearby cemetery - the other side of the long, yellow wall, on the street pointing the way to school each day. Those tales made it even more difficult to walk past it late at night. My brothers would take us out of the way to come home in another direction.

When we were young children, before his first car, my dad's means of transportation was a large bicycle. He would often take my sister and I on the rides to visit family and friends. We would both fit on the handlebar as he rode us around. Those were fun days.

Each year, despite any of the struggles encountered before, at Christmas, while we both fit on the handlebar, our Dad made sure that we had fun getting to that all-important police family Christmas party.

Christmas in Barbados serves up warm nights, and we would all look forward to either a walk, or a bicycle handlebar ride to the party. We saw that as the gift, a party, a warm night, smiles, laughs, and a toy that was not homemade. It was a gift treasured all year long.

As we grew older, he would take us to the beach on early weekend mornings for that sunrise 'dip' in the ocean. This was a time when native islanders would meet up and talk long before the tourists would appear. As quiet conversation floated across the sand, the frigid waters lay, calm, awaiting the warming from a rising sun.

It was more than a weekend jaunt. It was tradition tied to health, and some part of health is always tied to community and connection. The coming tourists disturbed those early traditions. They didn't see the sunrise as a healer, or its marriage with the waves, as a way to be restored before starting a new day. The sea water cures many ailments, as does family.

We would be back home in time for breakfast and that day's trip to the market. We would be back before mom would begin to demand the start of daily chores.

FAMILY

We grew up as a large family, sharing everything, and letting nothing go to waste. The family's abundance of fruits was traded for whatever plenty neighbors possessed. We ate from the land and from the sea. Strong in old practices established for generations, the 'sweetbreads' and 'great-cakes' were reserved for visiting guests.

The African traditions of supporting the village, and accepting its support, were fundamental roles our parents took on. Our 'close-in' village grew as our parents embraced caring for a grandmother, and for my mother's young sister. My aunt was married, with a growing family, and had a total of six children: all except one, was younger than my mother's youngest - me.

Despite our lack of many things, we never went hungry, always had shelter, and always had clothes made to wear. Toys were handmade: boxcarts, rolling tires, etc. There were microcosms inside microcosms - small island, group, fish aplenty, flour and fruit for all.

My parents practiced their faith in God, and, they showed it in actions. In this way, we led a simple life; church every Sunday, service to others, and sharing what little we had. Sometimes, that meant "taking from Peter to pay Paul".

One of our cousins, Rita, was embraced by our parents who adopted her, formally, and raised her with us - as a sibling. Even her name was changed so that she could be part of any travels and triumphs we might come upon. God and family were, and are, first.

Feeding and clothing all of us was a challenge for my parents. It meant groceries on credit from the city store, homemade dresses for mum and us girls. It even meant that Dad would tailor suits for himself and my brothers.

In early morning, the bakery would cast its smells out like a net.

We arrived purposely late in the afternoon; we were there for the 'day-old bread', or even bread two days old.

Flying Fish, practically the official native food of the island, were cheap. Mum could combine the bargain of ten fish for a dollar, with the harvest of our own backyard breadfruit tree. We ate simply. We ate well.

Then there were too many of those steaming meals; and, now there are too few.

The smells, while those meals were cooking, will ever be a reminder of home, of personal history. The smells are remembrance and hope - good, salty, steamy-wet.

Flying Fish and "cou-cou" (made from cornmeal or steamed breadfruit) was survival food, but we had it plentifully, and it was always made with love.

CHATTEL

Bridgetown Barbados had rich and poor enclaves. Ours was somewhere in-between.

Chattel homes were every dot on the map of our space in the city. Yet, Chattel was not a word given much thought by young girls, or even by the parents of the neighborhood.

We lived in huddles of houses named after the position our ancestors held. They were chattel, property, things to be bought, sold, and traded. When outright slavery was banned, those freed had to rent use of the land from the former slaveholders.

Sharecropping is not a 'US-only' nightmare.

Should a family need to move from one landholder's plantation to that of another, there was no other accommodation other than taking the house with you. The original Chattel homes were smoothed logs worked to hold together without nails. The entire home could be disassembled and carted to a new location.

Then, an entire family would share a single flat roof covering a single room. A more prosperous family, or a very large family, might afford two of the Chattel shacks. When connected such a family would have two roofs: 'two gables' and a flat kitchen portion.

Whether it was of necessity, or prosperity - as measured in our neighborhoods - two roofs, two gables, in the clutter of homes stood out.

The Chattel home enclaves evolved to permanent neighborhoods of solid wooden homes, in the style of those before. The wood was faced with stone; first the front, with a gradual, affordable progression toward the rear sections.

Our home was the usual "Chattel" Barbadian home with 2 'gables' and a flat portion containing the kitchen.

Everyone we knew had Chattel homes. Some remained wood; others were replaced with stone, in part or entirely over time. There were competing front gardens with Crocus plants. There were breadfruit and coconut trees in the back.

With all that plenty, a girl could still wish for more; like the dark green under a deep blush of red freckles that the fruit on a shared mango tree displayed.

Every year there were changes and renewal, some with comforting predictability. Easter and Christmas meant new, white stones would be added to the paths created for water run-off. Often a fresh coat of paint would perk up the contrasting windows.

Our two gables formed the home first visible when rounding the corner onto the street. Mum sewed newly embroidered drapes so light as to float in and out of the windows with the breeze. The house was alive, teasing and winking in the warm, steady breeze of a Bridgetown morning.

Inside, nine of us went about the rituals of readying for the day. The parents were steady and practiced at organizing the four boys and three girls.

I was the last.

Cared for by all, I was avoided by two. With seven children, in a small space, inevitably my mother would call out - "take your sister along with you".

When it rained we stayed inside. We lay in bed, and listened to the fat drops of rain sound tiny, flat explosions against the galvanized roof.

There were three bedrooms spaces. We three girls shared a bed. The four boys did the same. As the older siblings ventured to other parts of the island or the world, it seemed as though that closeness never changed. When an older sister moved to England, her space in our room was taken by an adopted cousin; a new sister.

The two-gabled stone house, with the white stone bed we made for the water to run away, was always full and warm. The breeze always flirted with mum's embroidered curtain magic. The steel of the roof always gave us shelter, and even music in the rain.

CRICKET

Outside of school (and not counting the forays into the city my brothers paid us to keep secret) we had only two other worlds. There was church. There was our cozy, stone, two-peaked home.

Everyone we knew looked like us. Everyone was not us.

Raised as non-denominational Christians, we kept to ourselves. Strict rules, strict activities. Church every Sunday.

Outside of our little stone home, with the contrasting windows, and the licking embroidered drapes, there was the wall. The yellow wall of the cemetery had played another part in our lives.

The four rocket-like turrets that were the corners of the cemetery were connected by the wall that led to school. Equally important, the wall led into town. There, in that place, was another way of life.

The "in-between" of getting to town was peopled by everyone like us, and those not like us. There was a world that came to life at various times, an "in-between" world, the world of cricket.

In that world, outside some of the rum shops in other neighborhoods, our look did not set us apart. There, all neighborhood types were represented.

We all gathered around the radio to hear the cricket matches. The connection was instant. Even if the participants didn't think about it, the same gatherings were taking place in Jamaica, England, India, and South Africa. We were connected.

Cricket was the sport of the nation. The uncanny ability of Gary Sobers to win for the West Indies made him a legend. People talked about him as though they knew him, as though nothing would ever be better than for him to show up as the dust of the day settled on the small tables outside the rum shops. Nothing would be better than debating a match with the legend himself, and to take the measure of the real man in our own place. Men listened to matches in the rum shops, backyards, and on front steps - all gathered around the radio- nothing else mattered during game season.

Rum shops, bakeries, buses speeding their turns in the roundabouts, and women selling peanuts on balanced head trays, that was town. The pungent smell of a lively market was punctuated by the sharp crack of a machete splitting coconuts. The sweet aroma of cakes and turnovers was consuming. This was town.

Town was excitement, and promise, and cheese cutters, and fish cakes. It was the beauty of the surprise, assaulting clash of car exhaust with the wandering smell of freshly fried fish you could not see. Town was the place to be. But not on a school day.

Friday nights were magical to hear, and smell. There was Bajan grilled fish, calypso music and loud domino games. The neighborhood rum shops let 'island sounds' drift out to draw both locals and tourists.

Temptation sometimes won out, even in strict households. Older brothers would deliver bribes to keep quiet about them floating off into the streets to sample the promise that nights in the town could deliver. There was always the cost of the bribe, and there was always the harsh cost and dread of being found out.

Temptation often won.

Too young to do more than collect bribes, we young girls stayed home and were entertained by the sounds carried on the night breezes.

We had our own private DJ; right across the street. At sunset the music started - sounds of Mighty Sparrow, Harry Belafonte, and many more. Thin walls and open windows were friendly to our imaginations. Young girls stayed at home, but free music could fly through any window like the small night birds that were only a flash past the eye, and a whoosh when the nights were bright with the moon.

THE WALL

5:00 a.m. It is still dark outside. No "duppy"-ghosts came last night; that means we had no visits from spirits from the past that preferred the night winds. Again, it is time for school. Again, the day outside would start with the walk past the wall.

On the first glimpses of an orange sky, low against the horizon, the signal of an early sunrise calmed the fear of walking past the wall in the dark. No ghosts traveled in the light.

The dark was the time the "duppy"-ghosts took for themselves. It was time taken from us, from the living, from flesh. And, a wandering young mind could imagine them a jealous, selfish, naked lot. The sun drove them to their damp, dark homes and pulled tired bones and anxious youth from the ones above ground.

There were pleats in uniforms, striped neckties, and colors abounding. The bright, white shirts were framed in the carefully chosen hues that were the brand of a school or church.

The only white shirt will be worn yet another day. Washed and ironed by the last one to bed the night before; the tired mum.

The heat met the ordinary pavement and came up with an everyday magic. There was air you could see shimmer, tease, and curve the street and trees ahead. Bridgetown Barbados is a hot place.

The way to school was well trod and well known. The wall that was part of the journey was two blocks long, but seemed more like a mile. Faded yellow, in need of repair, the wall seemed a lot taller than any souls walking in its shadow. The end-caps, its corners, were high cylinders, like some poor empty church with only one color of flat stained glass. They resembled rockets tied to the corners of an enormous green kerchief that was the cemetery inside those chipping yellow walls.

The wall was part of every day, even when it did not need to be touched. Dragging fingers along it each day, on the way to the school bus, somehow raised hope that friction would slow the inevitable.

Just beyond the end of the cemetery block was a school for girls who took delight in tormenting anyone not like them, not dressed like them; they were not above beating anyone they saw as weaker, or an enemy.

Dragging fingers across the chipping petals of yellow paint was a connection that, perhaps, could toughen, make harder hands. Perhaps vulnerability could be rubbed away.

Perhaps, there was strength to be drawn from those that lay on the other side of the wall.

Every day there was the walk on this yellow side of the cemetery wall. Every day the duppy-ghosts failed to rise up into the sunshine as a shield against horrid girls and, even more, from uncertainty.

One girl was small, with thin bowed legs, and five thick course braids. They were columns of imagination, or fear, escaping her head. Those braids were twisted at home with love. Those braids appeared to reach for the sky, when they were not used as targets for attacks that spun the girl in circles, tossing her to the ground to collect a few scars that were painful, but never so deep as the scars within.

That girl was me.

She was the version of me who had to choose between waiting for the duppy-ghosts to rise and defend, or choose to follow her braids, her imagination, to the sky and beyond. Young girls, especially ones unsure, ones hurt, imagine much.

ISLAND SCHOOL DAYS

It was the late 1960s. It was Bridgetown. Not many were spared being part of the tumult that was covering near and far like the shadow of an eclipse. Even the youngest were given deep lessons in the uglier sides of colorism, and in class politics.

Siblings had gone before and fought before. Parents fought battles unseen. Everyone knew that our world, our street of Chattel houses, our church, our home was not a flowered hippie haven. Our flowers were witness to struggles sometimes deep, and often painful.

My father would fight for any of us. As the youngest, I enjoyed the benefits of his well-practiced opening of doors, or the unquestioning provision of shelter, physical and emotional. Most probably, we were sheltered from truths and harms even when we did not know it.

Around the time one turns thirteen one of the sortings, in race and class and schools and school-child economics, occurs. When my turn came there were choices.

One of the best girls' schools was not far away from our home. It was one of the places for the smartest. I had proven that mastering academics was within my grasp. I looked forward to new crisp white blouses and dreamed about the new school's colors. Everyone would know what I had accomplished. My parents would be proud.

This girls' school was also a place where no one was darker than a paper bag. My family was not in that class.

My father made sure that his shirt was crackling with starch and white as the highest clouds on the hottest day. His constable's uniform was a different type of armor on that day.

We appeared at the girls' school, stoic and standing rod stiff. We did not say much to one another. All I knew was that what happened would change my life. My father, Constable Lacey Scantlebury, knew the value of the battle ahead, and he knew the odds.

I don't remember if my hand was held, only that it was wet and trembling. We walked in through the solid pillars that were a reminder that such a place was a fortress. The girls' school was a great castle that kept dark Black girls out and light brown girls with money hidden inside.

My father fought for me; for me to be judged on what my brain proved it could do. This battle, behind the great fences and walls of the stone school, went against us.

The system was not built to tolerate changes to its social rules; rules that could be altered at-will.

The lesson was learned. The rules can be changed by whoever controls the game.

I remain proud of the fight my father fought for me. The cruelest defeats are often those tossed out at the whim of another. Sometimes those defeats can be turned to advantage. For me, the one advantage was that the next best alternative for my schooling would put me in the St. Andrews parish on the north side of the island.

The Alleyne School was there, and my brother had already matriculated. We would take a bus together to spend our days far from our small stone-fronted home and the familiar smells of my mother's cooking.

The bus, and getting to the bus, were the first challenges of every day. Together, we would take the long walks past the cemetery to get to the bus stop. This is where the kids gathered for the different buses to their respective schools. We could not afford to be late.

I could not afford to give in to fears of what was behind the long yellow wall, or in front of me - the other girls' school, a future that was not the dream of being the same as those behind the walls and fences at that girls' school. The poking paint chips, yellow-painted back to near their place in the last season held only a little of me behind each day. The rest, I carried with me, and do.

The way to school was a long ride from Bridgetown, in early morning, on open 'church-seat style' buses each day. The bus gasped and chortled its aging growls beneath our hard benches as it was brushed, scratched, and whipped by sugarcane leaves.

The branches, stalks, and leaves did not spare any of us not quick enough to lean in as the school bus tore through the hills. On rainy days, the canvas protectors would be unfurled on the open sides of the bus. The open seats were a place for those too adventurous for the safer inner seats. The canvas was tightened over the end bars, and those game for challenging the weather would venture from under it.

Wet or dry, inner or outer seats, riders all shared racing hearts as the bus careened over the roads. Sometimes, the speeds were so great that we could barely grab breath from the rushing air that was all but a shout of 'danger'.

The bus whipped around hillsides where there were no sidewalks. Somehow the driver kept the slipping wheels braced to the road's edge and away from the deep ditches that beckoned the uninitiated to dark gullies. We said nothing and all thought the same things.

If the ride was laughable, it would have been raucous laughter. There would have been slapping of knees, at the speeds we barreled. It was not some coughing guffaw; it was a grab for life, holding on to the parts you did not want to lose. Each day, at those speeds, under the sway of the thin metal capsule that was our transport to a world just beyond Bridgetown, we would arrive at school with time to play a little before classes.

Each day, uniformed, pressed, and preened we gathered in the courtyard for morning prayer and the Headmaster's greeting before studies.

Each day, during my first year at the Alleyne School, the tall shadow that was my brother loomed over me, offering protection against the rituals inflicted on new students. I would be an exception.

In the second year, I found my own light, blossomed and flourished.

The uniform was the same for all the girls, and I was determined to make my accomplishments, my new skills, help me to stand out. As with being academically qualified to attend the girls' school, my best weapon, my only weapon, was how far ahead I could prove myself in things fairly measured. I used my only tool.

The Alleyne School was a sanctuary and a private practice place to audition new things to challenge me. Those new challenges were far beyond skin color, money, and the size of a parent's house. I found the joys of art productions, and Shakespeare found me when I learned to listen.

The influence of the British dominated the classroom study selections: scripture, British history, Latin, English literature.

Sports such as high jump, track and relays as well as javelin and discus were encouraged as areas in which to excel for inter-school competitions. Beyond this were inter-island competitions, and winners were sent off to world competitions. Everyone seemed to have long legs, always in front, lunging forward, winning. Everyone ran.

Everyone competed. In every subject, we all competed. In nearly every class subject, standing out was all about successful descriptive writing.

Multiple choice testing was non-existent. Even in mathematics, there were four to six complicated questions. Success was understanding the numbers, but also in critical thinking - how to convey one's process and result. We even competed in communication.

In a class, using the essay as a teaching and learning tool, I was asked to write about 'My Career'. I learned more about 'me' than I learned about how to use the essay as a communication tool.

A career where I could be my own boss was critical. Being able to learn more about why an illness had taken a sister from me so early in life was critical. I could not help her (as I could not help my father help me with the battles at the girls' school), but I could learn enough, and go far enough, to help others.

My career would be in medicine. I would be a doctor. I would help others as I was not in a position to help my sister.

Our family doctor in Barbados was tall and white, with a British accent. He helped others. He had answers. He made us well. I imagined a world where all the patients were mine. I would be the one helping them.

I dreamed of making my parents proud of me and sure that their effort in launching me toward 'more' was worth the work.

From behind, my parents pushed. Always at my sides, they protected. From within, my dreams drove me forward.

As a doctor, I could be the heroine of many life-stories, and the topic of admiring essays.

A few beyond my family encouraged me to consider going far beyond the stations associated with dark-skinned girls with thin legs, and proud thickets of black hair.

THE PLAN, THE LOSS, MY PLAN

Expectations were high for all of the seven children of our household. There were no excuses, no absences from classes unless a hurricane was coming. Teachers had spanking liberties. There was no ambiguity about the importance of making the most of school - school for learning, not school as a social exercise.

Education was THE number one priority and task. We were not alone in striving. Achieving a near one-hundred percent literacy rate for the island was a national goal.

Mum went ahead to New York alone to prepare a life for the rest of us. My parents realized that for us to achieve our greatest potential we would have to leave our beloved island for a place with more opportunities. I was twelve and the youngest. We were capable of contributing to the wellbeing of the family, and assist our father in maintaining order at home. As we grew older, more responsibility was assigned to us.

Despite the difficulty of not having our mother at home with us, we knew it would not be long before we would all be together again. With time, we left our home behind for new opportunities: first Michael, then the girls.

The reunion was complete when Ronald and my Dad made the trip from Bridgetown to New York City.

It was a new nexus for our family, New York. It was the screech of cab brakes and subway wheels, the smell of melting asphalt and the sounds of curses hung in the air for fun. There were no backyard breadfruit trees, and mangoes only came from stores. New York was gray, and one learned that only tourists look up, so blue sky is there but only used by dreamers and children. I was both.

My sister Mary met all of the expectations. She also was the reason for much of my curiosity about medicine. Her death made me sad; it also planted the seed whence came my plan. I could not be her savior, but I could be the heroine doctor.

She followed the family plan, and forged a path outside of our small island. She left Barbados at age 19, traveling to England to study nursing. I was only six when she left.

I knew that she was going on a grand adventure to a place whose description sounded other-worldly to me. My mother would emphasize that Mary was going away to study, not to explore London. Yet, all that I heard of London, how different it was than Bridgetown made me think otherwise.

At six, I imagined that Mary would instantly become a nurse. I imagined that she would always wear her white uniform and perfectly bright white, unscuffed shoes. I imagined that she would have a hat that identified her as a nurse, as someone needed.

In my thoughts, there would be thousands of Britons walking on crowded streets where dust was not a problem. My sister would stand out with smooth, dark brown, oiled skin in her white, starched uniform and nurse's hat. In those same thoughts, she would stroll from her hospital to her own small flat, picking up fish and chips wrapped in newspaper along the way. She could look down from her window onto the sidewalks as the flow of people became a trickle, the sun would cast longer shadows, and her radio told her news from even more exotic parts of the world. And, I imagined that she would think of me and mum and dad and plan to have me visit.

The reality was that Mary went to England to study. Her focus was on becoming a nurse and the betterment and respect it would provide. She followed the family plan. She used her inheritance of determination. Two years later, her life was, unexpectedly and unfortunately, cut short.

My sister Mary died at age twenty-two, from complications of an infection. Today that would have been preventable.

Her success was a bright flash, cut short. My memory of her was as much imagination as it was reality. Yet, her true legacy, for me, was an even further awakening of my curiosity.

I wanted to know why she died at such a young age. I wanted to know how it could have been avoided. As I grew older, the irony of her death, juxtaposed with her profession, filled me with even more determination.

News of Mary's initial illness was conveyed by telegram from England. This came a few days before her death. Vivid memories still remain of the arrival of the second telegram delivered by the 'motorcycle man' as he was called. You heard his clunky, noisy machine before it rounded the corner into sight.

The day before the second telegram, Mum's wedding ring turned black. She knew the sign. Later that day, 2 doves sat on the flat roof of the house and cooed, until they were chased away.

The night before was rough for all. Mary's two dogs, left with us at home, refused to be quieted as their spirits sensed her demise long before the telegram arrived.

Their howls could not be tamed by hugs or indoor sanctuary. Cold baths did not break their anguish as her soul drifted from the hills and dales and concrete canyons of England, to the shores of Barbados. Her dogs sensed her. Our mother knew too.

Our sleepless mother rose with the sun and took a seat at the side window. She waited for the telegram.

The puttering of the old motorcycle as it approached our home the next morning brought the written confirmation of her death. Dad, given instructions to be home before the news arrived, rode up as the officer was dismounting. He took the envelope.

Neighbors heard the howls of pain and sorrow that escaped from our parents. The sky would cast dark clouds to match the sadness of the day. Those close to us came to comfort and embrace us, as we watched our father, broken but suffering, explain what we already knew. It was his duty as our father.

We now lived with a mother who never had a chance, or the means, to visit her firstborn even in death. She had to give the task of burying her child to someone else; someone four thousand miles away, with a generous heart.

So much, it was sure, was gone.

A young life, was cut short by death, in a place all unknown. There was no family, no love close by, to embrace her beyond aloneness as she departed this world. We mourned our loss together for a few days before resuming our back to school routine.

Soon after Mary died, brother Kenrick left for England. Denied a visa during the year of our tragedy, he would be granted permission 2 years later. That opened the door for the quick departure of our brother David. While I did not get to know them until I was much older, and they had both moved on from England, they showed that the path to the world beyond Barbados was viable.

Kenrick left Bridgetown, explored England and what it had to offer for education and employment, and eventually settled in Canada. David also emigrated to England before finding his place in New York. It would be many years before we would see them again.

Our mother turned her energy into entrepreneurship. She was a cake decorator, a seamstress, and all-around homemaker.

LANGUAGE PATH

The lines of my family's travels, if drawn on a globe, form a strange and beautiful flower. When I imagined it then, and think of it now, it is a clear set of paths to a 'world of options'.

Mary, and my brothers, used England. I could use New York, or England, or Canada, or even a return to Barbados. Uncles created paths to Panama, Liberia and even America. And, no one eliminated applying skills and effort to the continent of Africa, to connecting the African Continent to America, to Asia. Options and opportunities lay before those who worked to make opportunities; opportunities beyond those that existed at home.

Each place, where my older siblings studied, and traveled, and lived used English as the mother-tongue. Language, and all the work in critical thinking and expository writing, was a key to success. The foundation had been laid by the rigorous school demands. The places where a doctor could use the English language would be keys for me also.

BROOKLYN

My first stop outside of Bridgetown was Brooklyn. It claimed to be, to reflect, my whole country. It was also a dark, tasty stew of Black people - from everywhere. Brooklyn was a conglomerate of nationalities from the West Indies and South America to the continent of Africa. The smells of barbequed ribs, fresh baked bread and curried goat filled the air along the avenues.

Cold, and icy, was our new Brooklyn home. Our first-floor home was known as a 'railroad apartment'; there were few windows, and none were opened. The teasing flaps and licks of the homemade drapes flying in and out of our Bridgetown 'two- gabled' home were long gone.

In Brooklyn, the windows were kept closed, blocking out the outside noise, fumes, and smells of yesterday's meals. In Brooklyn, we looked to heavy curtains to block winter's cold air - the new climate, weather and the brick and concrete big city.

Spring meant an impending summer with awakening trees and the sound of birds and the return of the less hearty pigeons. Some of the black and gray and white pigeons did not hide during the winter. They were pets, carefully housed on tar roofs; rain, snow, or sunshine.

Darkness came much later in the summer than it did in Barbados. Ice cream trucks, block parties, and Coney Island rides lifted us above the boredom of the hot summer.

When the heat was too much to bear, we would welcome the open hydrants and relished the spray of cool water. The city had long-before learned that cooling the people in the streets was important enough to commit it to law. We had a right to the summer spray, and to play on a wet, cooler street. We used that right.

Brooklyn was the United States, was New York, and was the West Indies. It was a rude awakening from our sleepier, calmer

Bridgetown Barbados. In Brooklyn, there were connected houses; there was little grass, and the playing fields were the overgrown feet of long-gone buildings. Brooklyn had no coconut or mango trees, had no God-given sustenance growing nearby, no breadfruit. Gardens and flowers were pots on sills.

Manhattan was only miles away, and it was galaxies away. The way to get there was a subway train that was 40 stair steps up-in-the-air. It creaked, cracked, moaned, and squealed. I am sure it learned from all that it saw. I am sure it never told any of the secrets discovered.

Our subway experience was much the same, creaking, moaning, squealing, and telling all of what we saw each day.

Turnstiles, in the New York Subway System, are obstacles and art. They require effort and time to master. Young girls, rude adventurous boys, and the defiant learned to wiggle to the other side - fast as deception, deft as art - and, ne'er to be caught. At least, that was the goal.

Timing was key. I would watch those 'artful dodgers'. They would make sure to finish the mounting of the stairs to our elevated train stop just as the first cars arrived. They would 'wiggle the turnstile', and slip, quick as a flash, from the breached turnstile into the train at the last second before the train's door was about to close.

Those boys and girls, of course not me, made it a daily adventure, pure art, the stuff of legend. None of that glory was possible if you did not arrive at the base of the station on time. It was a slightly dangerous game to race the heart on a cool morning, two stories above an awakening street in the Brooklyn of that time.

We lived in that area of Brooklyn even after we all were united.

Dad eventually found a job at Merrill Lynch in N.Y. working in security. He had no gun, but that was no problem for him.

He rose at three thirty a.m. every weekday for that job. He maintained a ritual: meditation, bible inspiration, and then lunch preparation. He left for his daily train ride to Wall Street each day, to begin his work at 7 am. He did not play the 'wiggle-and-dash' we teenagers relished. He was still our leader, our Constable Lacey Scantlebury. He was, simply, transplanted.

He never rushed, or got angry, when the train was late; or even when he was robbed. He was alive, blessed by God and thankful. New York, Brooklyn, was different - but still, in his mind, under the same God and rules of balance. We were fortunate to find friends from the same Church we attended in Bridgetown. Our practices were similar. We served the same God.

I, on the other hand, hated life and school in America. There was the coldness in neighbors, and ugly looks from foreign faces. That does not even mention the frigid temperatures we faced in the winter. Every US, New York, Brooklyn climate - physical, academic and social - was at every turn potentially cold.

High school was another rude awakening. There were no familiar essay competitions, just multiple choice testing. There was no emphasis on Shakespeare, no outside track fields, just a hardwood floor, high-ceilinged box - the gym. It was on the other side of Brooklyn: a train ride and a bus transfer each way. This would be my educational source for the next 3 years.

HIGH SCHOOL

Part of its name was "Prospect"; it was Prospect Heights High.

That lofty, hopeful, name was attached to my all-girls school with a bad reputation: robbery, molestation, extortion, and bribery. What a welcome to adolescent life in the United States. This was - Brooklyn.

It was 1973. Again, there were walls. There were rough truths on each side of the 'yellow wall' in Bridgetown - on one side duppy-ghosts and criminals hiding in the cemetery's night. On the other side, fingers dragging on the tenth layer of paint, trying to slow the advance of another encounter with mean girls, and ugly meetings with colorism and even intra-community classism.

At Prospect Heights High, there were the thick, red and white stone fortress walls. They, too, held back secrets and lies and held in opportunities and promise.

I learned to stay on the right side of the wall. Survival often depended on camaraderie.

Lynnette was Jamaican; she lived in our neighborhood and introduced me to others, like Janelle, also from Barbados. With similar backgrounds, we fought similar wars. Victory meant attending college. We were not going to allow the wall of rejection for being 'West Indian' curtail our ultimate desires for excellence. Whether it was our colorful fashion flair, the drawl of our native accents, or the simplicity of our hairstyles, we banded and braced, as a group, for the battles thrown our way.

I had my familiar, well-worn, and sharp weapons: over-achievement to remove all doubt, the discipline the crisp white blouse suggested, and curiosity. Biology Club, also known as Arista, and Pre-Med Club were paths to display a continued dedication and focus. I had not forgotten the big question about what did happen to, and what might have been avoided with, my departed sister Mary.

The library was the safe place. Shakespeare was an object of affection and endless re-readings, Julius Caesar in particular, brought joy and peace. Memories of my brothers playing their own version, uttering "Beware the ides of March" stirred my heart as I envision another brother falling to the ground, casting the famous line: 'Et tu, Brute?'

I reveled in the pages of books. Their pages have the power to intoxicate and to empower. A simple turn of a page can set free a wafting dry scent that can be a wide canyon of possibilities. From imagining the role of Mark Anthony embodied, to the eloquence of Hamlet's 'to be, or not to be' speech, each page had the power to enrapture, to make the mind cognizant of another time and place.

While there may be no single distinct scent attached to science, to mathematics, or to literature and art, there is always the beautiful scent of 'a story' as the book releases its secrets. The promise of story is that you will, always, leave with more than you had before.

CURB YOUR DREAMS !

Librarians are the kings and queens of those canyons of books, and pages, and possibilities. In those early times in Brooklyn the library royalty had 'some' power over my future. They were the guides. They were not always fair.

The librarian underappreciated my commitment to books and refused to allow me to check out any 'Literature' books. She believed that 'Literature' was beyond my level of comprehension. She refused to believe that someone like me could have read Shakespeare in the past. Those were books reserved for older students, she insisted.

"You would not understand what you are reading" she voiced while pointing me in the direction of the required readings of Jane Austen.

She knew nothing of my background. She did know how I looked.

I never allowed her to raise a wall. I had only one wall, the yellow wall. I would not allow her to block me; I was stronger.

My confidence was near boundless. I had overcome fear of the long, yellow wall in Bridgetown. I had triumphed in another place after the rejection at the girls' school. I had found friends and purpose and Shakespeare in Brooklyn.

I learned to avoid appearing too smart. That could, sometimes, result in being forced to be smart for someone else. That could mean doing work under another's name, and not telling the tale. It was all survival.

The goal had been set long before: attend, college, become a doctor. Nearing the end of my high school career in New York, it was time to make declarations, decisions, and applications.

My guidance counselor knew my academic record, but she did not know me. She overlooked my potential. To her, I had no promising future. The darkness of my skin blinded her, my Caribbean accent and quiet demeanor deceived her.

I was not one of her favorites!

Her idea was to tailor my future, based on what she knew to be a Black person's 'place'. It was a model embedded in her mind in the 1950s and early 1960s. That model was reflected in her fashion, demeanor and sense of superiority. The ruler she embraced every moment was in her mind the 'whip' she wished it to be.

I did not want to be at her mercy.

Her advice: "Get a job, and consider night school." To her, I was not 'college material'. I was an immigrant from another land, lacking the tools for a meaningful future. I was not worthy of her time or space.

COLLEGE - THE NEXT, OTHER, WORLD

No information was given, regarding types of colleges, to many who looked like me. We were kept ignorant to anything outside of New York.

Unflagging, as always, my parents insisted that I apply to college. I chose 2 local colleges - Barnard College in NYC, and Long Island University - the Brooklyn campus which was a few miles from home.

Blessed with a 4-year, full-ride academic scholarship to LIU, my financial concerns were eliminated. There would be no burden on my parents. Living at home was cheaper, and there would be opportunity to work some hours tutoring for extra income.

My confidence soared as I entered college. The freedom to excel was unleashed, releasing my innate abilities to absorb new levels of knowledge. Easily blending with the melting pot of students on campus, assimilation occurred with time and increased involvement.

The first semester I made the Dean's List. The joy on my dad's face will always be remembered as he equated that with striking gold. His youngest child, the first to attend college in the US, succeeded beyond all expectations. Excellence was demanded; and, excellence was attained. He was proud and became more so as the letters arrived each semester. He announced my accomplishments to all who would listen.

I majored in Biology/Premed as expected. My distaste for pithing frogs in Biology class did not deter Dr. Smith from mentoring me, and encouraging my pursuit of medical school. His glowing ebony hued skin, white teeth and dimpled cheeks were complemented by his rimless round glasses, always appearing to be precariously perched on the edge of his nose.

He held high expectations of excellence, demanded top performance and tolerated no excuses. He pushed each of us beyond our expectations.

With a greater purpose, I moved through my four years at Long Island University. Extra money obtained from tutoring and summer jobs in the corporate world, supported my extracurricular activities in photography. Sparked by an earlier elective in Photography Art class, I became enthralled with my new interest. Invited to participate in various competitions, I cherished mastering the art, and capturing images in a world that allowed for transformation in infinite ways.

It was a world I relished, like human life. It allowed for manipulation, like medicine, focusing on the details that matter. In every way, photography can capture life. Medicine can restore life.

The opportunity to engage in the art of photography opened up an opportunity for scholarship possibilities for medical school. I took advantage of this opportunity, applied and was rewarded a book scholarship: every dollar mattered. These experiences intensified my desire to return to the better-known jungle of academia.

AN ISLAND ACROSS EACH BRIDGE

Approaching graduation from LIU, the medical school application process was before me; and, it made me fraught with anxiety. The next steps, entering medical school, meant scaling walls - obstacles made up of steps and deadlines. On the other side there could well have been the equivalent of duppy-ghosts. It seemed that there were always souls waiting to spoil a lifetime dream.

Encouraged to apply to Meharry Medical School by my biology teacher and first mentor, I saw the wall shrink, just a little, as I received that first acceptance. Meharry Medical School accepted me - me - to join the incoming class. I floated instead of walking. Both distance, and location were uncharted by anyone I knew. I had come from Barbados. I had visited Washington D.C. The 'deep south' of Nashville Tennessee, the home of historically Black Fisk College and its legendary Meharry Medical School, was a thoroughly foreign and frightening orbit.

Unfamiliar with the South, I did not see how I would survive that far away from home. The history of the struggle by African-Americans in this country was as unknown to me as the promise and hollowness of the Emancipation Act.

Meharry was a Black medical school. It was storied, in its contributions to Black communities across the country. In the decades of years before, there were only two or three choices for a Black medical student. Meharry accepted me.

The real shock was my fear of venturing beyond the newly chartered waters of New York City. I was back to waiting.

I chose to await other options.

Soon, I heard from Yale University. The 'Wall' was shrinking more. I was excited; and, I still had an interview at Columbia University the next week.

I had only applied because a friend at church suggested I do so. In my mind, Columbia was beyond my reach, even though I had been accepted by Yale. I pondered the requirements for Yale, and my understanding of the need for thesis completion before graduation. I needed the constancy of intermittent exams which were fewer and less often than the standard medical school curriculum. I hesitated in returning my acceptance letter to Yale University.

The day of the interview at Columbia, hair was sprayed stiffly in place, prayers were sent up to heaven; ahead, the long ride stretched - Brooklyn to near the top of Manhattan, and part of the medical school world, Columbia's College of Physicians and Surgeons, 168th Street, New York, New York, USA.

It was December, and, that meant cold icy winds propelled from the Hudson River, between New Jersey and the rising bluff of granite that was Upper Manhattan. Any skin not tingling with fear was numbed by nature. I became aware that, I was unable to even know if my toes were still present. Despite it all, I felt comfortable, in control and hopeful.

The admissions office was on the first floor just beyond a revolving doorway. As I warmed myself from the outside chills, before entering the room, a calmness came over me. It was as if the stars were lined up in my favor.

My interview at Columbia University was exceptional, despite the cold windy day: hair stayed in place, answers were given with requisite confidence., Further armed with an excellent GPA, I felt, in my heart, that I would be accepted. The reference, Dr. Smith's recommendation, and his confidence in my abilities, was relayed with reassurance. His support was evident.

I was correct. The letter arrived, and I was able to float again. Excitedly, I accepted the invitation to join the Class of 1981.

FAITH

In the beginning, back in Bridgetown, nine of us lived in that two- gable chattel house

There was a guarantee of witnessing, or being part of, some barely controlled chaos. When those hectic mornings let us pour into the streets, we would often hear a softer music. We would hear: "Hi, Lacey."

My constable dad had an erect walk, a cordial manner, and a crisp uniform. He seemed 8 feet tall, head topped with the traditional black, red and sometimes white covered rigid hat, a British tradition still remaining. Black pants with a wide red strip down the side and ever shining black shoes completed the outfit.

He was a man of grace, patience, and wisdom, who taught us to: "trust in God, every step of the way .... "

" ... for without me, you can do nothing." John 15:5

Faith was ever-present in our thoughts; and, practicing our faith – demonstrably – was always to be act, or be part of the actions.

My faith in God has never wavered. My faith in myself often flagged.

There were tests at 'the Wall', and there were tests at other walls, even ones not visible to even those closest, those who 'didn't speak the language of the profession'. There were tests inside the pit of competition and hormones as powerfully thick and invasive as an entire high school. All this, unfortunate, human interaction could come from any angle - from teachers, librarians, and counselors who did not counsel.

"Trust in Him always" was my mantra. God was there for me. My family support was tremendous.

YOUR "A", OUR "C"

Getting into just one medical school is difficult. Getting into an Ivy League medical school can be nearly impossible. There were many options to consider,

For any U.S. born African-Americans, Meharry Medical School was considered "one of your own." Being labeled a "token", or being virtually slapped with the opinion that "your own" schools accept most who applied, are both bruising experiences. I was learning that knowledge and excellence can be elevated or crushed by the color of your skin. I learned that, while the M.D. and license earned look the same to some patients, the degree and connections made if one survived an Ivy League medical school would likely go further. I still had the plan formatted around helping others avoid the pain my sister's death had brought.

Those students, who did not share my accent or skin color, used their 'entitlement' to do their undergraduate work at Yale or at Columbia, or at Brown. Their work there mattered. Their 'B grades' and 'High C grades' mattered more than each LIU 'A'.

I was missing an 'entitlement'. But, I was missing no achievement or understanding. Intelligence, and drive, can overcome and trump entitlement. I proved my intelligence and drive. Leaping over the wall to join those who also had entitlement proved to be more than a simple challenge.

My newly adopted nation-home, the U.S., entrusted its governance, health, and education systems to those who emerged, unscathed, from its class-maze, and connections-entitlement driven system of walls.

I was an interloper. I was 'in', but not a part.

TOKENS

The day I received my letter of acceptance from Columbia College of Physicians and Surgeons (P&S, they called it), I took the letter to my classes at LIU. I rode the elevator up to the Dean's office. I danced my way across the hall, and, I barely entered before blurting out my good news.

Disappointment was visible on the face of the Pre-Med office counselor: the favorite Caucasian student did not get admitted to Columbia P&S. I did.

"How come you got accepted and Jane didn't?" The obvious, ugly, question was finally spoken aloud.

Rationalizing my admittance to both Yale and Columbia, as a Black student, was almost easier for them to digest.

I remember something along the lines of: "Columbia just needed to fill their 'quota' for the number of minorities accepted. So, you probably were selected to be a token".

I was chosen, but as a 'token Black'.

Perhaps that was true. It didn't matter. My outcome would be the same as I had been resolute about achieving it for a lifetime. I'd take it, and I did. In four years I was going to be a doctor.

I turned and left the office, my excitement now gone, a wave of resentment and anger rising from my core.

Already, I had learned the basics of discerning one's self from other; that is, except my family. I had learned that the rules, like histories, are written by the victors. I learned that sometimes those true histories are long, sometimes silent, and almost always painful in chronicling the battles between races and classes.

My brief explorations of full trust in others yielded mixed results. In the case of befriending my college classmate Dana, the reward was tremendous. In the case of looking at how the world viewed me only some experiences were positive. Dana was an exceptionally smart student from Syria. Tall, with a heavy Syrian accent, she likely, shared the same feelings of rejection by those around us. She also wanted to be a doctor. I wanted to have her 4.0 GPA. We were different, but for us the 'walls' were common obstacles.

Even as a very young woman I learned that there would never be absolute equality in how someone like me was judged. Some of the elders, even those U.S. born, were treated the same. We all came to this side of the oceans in slave ships. A landing in Virginia, or a landing in the West Indies changed nothing for them or us, their descendants.

We had to be better, and perform above 'first-class', and we would still be treated as second or third-class.

I knew that my goal, my destiny, was reachable. Walls and duppy-ghosts would rise, and could be felled. Each battle would produce disappointment - just by its existence. But with each battle, better weapons, even simple ones, can be forged to win victories over rivals. Each triumph over those obstacles can be a joyful success.

This was true for all the Danas of the world. It was true for me.

For those of us that persevered, for me, the earned diploma would never show the word 'token'. It would, simply, read DOCTOR IN MEDICINE.

A DIFFERENT MANHATTAN PROJECT

While in the throes of the undergraduate experience, little attention was paid to the value of an "A" at LIU compared to a "C" in the Ivy Leagues.

I was proud to be in medical school. I was the first of my generation to attend a full, four-year college. I was the first, of my generation, to achieve entry into an Ivy League medical school. I was propelling my family forward, where it wanted to go.

In many ways Columbia College of Physicians and Surgeons (P&S) 'was' Manhattan – to me. The Medical School was a world floating far, far above the gnarled, gray and brown pebbles embedded in concrete paths, and walls, laid a century before.

In Upper Manhattan, the 'people' walked those pebbly sidewalks on the way to support a city that did not acknowledge them as citizens. I was only one group away from being 'unrecognized' by the America of the United States.

No one – no one – can take on Manhattan Island, NYC. You can enter, submit, rage, explore, slither, wonder and wander.

Manhattan is endless. Manhattan is only fourteen miles long.

At its fat waist, Manhattan is only two miles wide. More than two million people live there. More than 4 million people work there each day.

Manhattan is a rock. There are few soft places.

Being part of the Columbia College of Physicians and Surgeons meant submitting to Manhattan. You huddle, together, sheltering one another from the lack of a rain or money. Landlords, barely contained, are kings. Nothing is free; no breadfruit in Brooklyn, no breadfruit in Manhattan. Not even the applause spawned by a new height of achievement is given for free.

Manhattan is competition beyond anything imagined in Barbados schools.

I was a master of achieving 'A' grades in Barbados, at Prospect High, and at Long Island University.

Mastery at each level, in each organization works only in that place. One can train, can learn, and can project for a specific outcome. I believed I was prepared for Columbia's College of P & S, because I was over-prepared for my experiences at Long Island University.

I was wrong.

Adapting new study habits, I had to learn fast how to make it in a new system.

The intensity was high. We were all smart and knowledgeable. Medical school demanded a greater depth of commitment and fortitude than college.

Group study sessions, notes exchanges, practice exams; these were all tools. Ultimately, it was reaching deep within for confidence and extra brain power that would prove successful.

The program followed the tried-and-true standard: two straight years of courses followed by two years of clinical rotations. The challenges of biochemistry and pharmacology were almost insurmountable, but all I needed was to pass.

There were days when I felt I would not make it. I wanted to give up. On my drive to Brooklyn I would practice my explanation for quitting before I reached home.

Despite my practiced excuses, failure was not acceptable in our household. The reassurance I needed, from family, from home, from my village - packaged with abounding love and hope, would always buoy me enough to return to school.

Each time, with my confidence restored, and possessing even more determination to succeed, I went back to Manhattan and behind the walls of the medical school.

Short trips to Brooklyn meant home cooked food for our group and my dad's famous coconut bread.

We looked forward to that bread, all of us helping it make its rounds in Bard Hall.

BARD HALL

Bard Hall was home for all of us the first year of medical school. Not privileged to have a room facing the Hudson River, there were no romantic views. There were, though, cold winds from the wide, cruel waters that separated our part of Manhattan from the Palisades of New Jersey. Across that river, from our new home in Bard Hall, there were people not frayed with worry. There were people not struggling with sheaves of notes, all too flimsy to offer protection from the horrors of surprise tests.

The extra classes I had taken in college to better prepare me and give me those added advantages were covered in the first weeks of class.

I loved my time at Long Island University, and the feeling that my many accomplishments there provided. The preparation, though, paled in comparison to the challenges I now faced in the Ivy League.

I felt defeated and not at all above the pack. The intensity of the medical school curriculum was as a shock wave; it demanded more than my full attention. It demanded complete immersion and submission to each task, each class, each test. Perhaps the deficiencies I faced were somehow related to my pre-college habits, or years of not being pushed to the highest bar. Regardless of the reasons, it now required new techniques to study, to maintain information recall, and to work collectively with my classmates, facing similar but different issues. We collaborated with our notes, offered support to each other and drove each other through late night repetitive drills before each exam.

With a dislike for coffee, my caffeine boost came via uncountable cans and bottles of cola; strong enough to ward off sleep until at least 2 AM. Pass, fail, or honors were the options. I had to believe in my abilities, knowing that God had brought me this far for a reason. "I've got this."

Phil 4:13. 'I can do all things through Christ who strengthens me.'

TEN PLUS TEN

Our class had 148 students, with 20 being Black or Latino. Within the group of 10 Latinos, the backgrounds ranged from Puerto Rico to various Latin countries in South America.

Within each ethnic group, there were five males and five females. Perhaps the school anticipated potential relationships; equal pairing possibilities. I have not, still, drawn a conclusion about how deep the connection between the two groups of ten should be, or was supposed to be.

What I do know is that the medical school grind fostered building relationships - ones of friendship, and - ultimately - for survival of all participating parties. We stuck together to offer support, class notes, and an emotional presence when things seemed hopeless.

As the shock and relief of completing the first year wore off, we adjusted to the new and different ways of learning, and were grateful that the year came to a close without any major failures.

To celebrate, we opted for a group vacation during our first and only free summer. Four of us from our class set out for Hawaii: three females and one male. We all shared the same room, but while others had eyes on Valentino, we three were there just to relax and unwind.

The package deal was for ten days, including hotel and airfare. That, we could afford. What we could not afford was to eat three meals a day at Hawaiian hotel prices. There was eating, and there was running out of money. We did both.

Buffet breakfast included a large travel bag that could carry away any extra croissants and fruits not already cut. We did that.

There were free dinners at the expense of hotels or restaurants by pretending that some two of us were married or were considering purchasing a vacation timeshare. It was all in exchange for ninety minutes of lecture and a tour. We did that.

By the near end of our vacation, Valentino wanted little to do with us, vowing not another vacation without money. He had to find success in being a doctor.

As we moved through the struggles of memorizing the rigid book work and regurgitating that same material via written examinations, third year brought an opportunity to apply that retained knowledge to the clinical setting. Upper classmates offered tips on the best out-of-state or country opportunities we were offered as medical students. It was a chance to grow and learn new and different ways to practice medicine.

Andrea and I signed on to travel to Nigeria to assist in medical clinics; however, Africa was off limits as far as my family in Brooklyn was concerned.

There were rumors about rumors, with the facts long overlooked. I was not allowed to travel to Africa because Dr. Samuel Kountz had just returned from Africa and took ill in a Brooklyn Hospital. Dr. Kountz was known for performing a kidney transplant on live television in 1976 on the Today Show. He was also Chairman of the Department of Surgery at Downstate Medical Center.

While on tour in South Africa in 1977, Dr. Kountz contracted an illness that impaired him neurologically for the rest of his life. The word in Brooklyn was that he was bitten by an African Tsetse fly, and had become comatose. Armed with, and by, these false rumors, my parents refused to let me travel to Nigeria.

Dr. Kountz's illness was never diagnosed and he died after we graduated from medical school in December 1981. At the time of his death, he had performed about 500 kidney transplants, the most performed by any surgeon possibly at that time. He was an inspiration; and, what might have happened for my career in Nigeria will never be known.

Instead, I went to San Francisco to do a Radiology rotation, and to Barbados for Obstetrics and Gynecology. Andrea went on to Nigeria for a great experience.

WHICH WHITE COAT

First year gross anatomy class was played to a room filled with bodies donated to science or otherwise, preserved with formaldehyde, the smell of which permeated the entire room. Each 'cadaver' was assigned to groups of 4-5 students. Through our 'assigned bodies' we were to learn all the details of the human body. Mysteries lay in diagnosing what was removed when there were scars signifying previous operations.

From the first moment of dissection, I knew I wanted to be a surgeon. As we explored the various organ systems, from the muscular system and the tracing of each muscle to its tendinous connection, to the nervous system and how each nerve controls the said muscles, I remained in awe of the human body. The excitement of returning the next day or week to learn something anew drew me to the laboratory the night before. I aimed to be ahead of the pack.

I imagined myself operating on a living patient, removing the cancer such as that found in the abdomen of our 'Lucy", and see her recover and live a full life. I would be able to save her, something I was not able to do for my own sister.

I remained committed to a career in surgery. The exhilarating feelings returned as we moved from first and second year to the third year clinical rotations. It meant greater exposure with actual patients and the opportunity to be in the operating room.

I optimized my potential by increasing my presence on surgical rotations. It worked to solidify my focus on the goal of being a surgeon, in particular a general surgeon. The ability to correct a congenital abnormality in a child, or cure a disease by surgical resection was what I envisioned for the years to come.

Again, there were walls. An old obstacle of multiple-choice examinations at the end of second year arose, with the required Step 1 medical examination. Classmates were expressing the simplicity of the examination, suggesting that there was no need to study or prepare. This advice did not work in my favor, and I fell short of passing. Success was achieved with appropriate preparation. What worked for the majority, did not work for me. I had to learn the hard way; a fact I would store in my memory banks.

The new obstacles were every bit as daunting as the duppy-ghost cemetery wall in Bridgetown - but this new barrier was invisible to some.

There was no obvious beginning or end; yet, that wall was always before me. Despite my daily presence on some sub-specialties, near perfect patient presentations and participation on rounds, I struggled to gain the expected honors, reserved for some students despite their lack of routine attendance. The bias was often obvious, even to some non-Black students.

Fortunately, I earned honors ratings in my general surgery rotations. Granted an opportunity to work with Dr. Kenneth Forde, I was rewarded with an awesome and unprecedented opportunity to present a paper at the Surgical Forum. Even these offerings - to the too high, too wide wall ahead of me - were not enough to qualify me for a position as a general surgery intern. The new wall had a name - the "Surgical Match System".

My assigned preceptor at the time, a well-known plastic surgeon, refused to recommend me for a position in general surgery. I "did not have what it took" to be a surgeon.

He suggested to me that it would be best if I considered a "less challenging" career, one I could easily handle.

He saw me as a dermatologist, or perhaps a podiatrist. Even pediatrics was within the realm of what he thought I should consider. But, according to him this young West Indian girl was, perhaps, trying to 'punch above her weight'.

I loved my rotation in general surgery and was determined to be a surgeon. Having received excellent evaluations from the residents in charge, I was immensely disappointed in the preceptor's attempt to clip my wings, to limit my options.

Perhaps I had paid little attention to the female residents already pursuing their quest to be general surgeons. The unhappiness and discontent they faced frequently from older staff surgeons, was often, quite evidently, discriminatory. They advised against a career in surgery. Struggling to gain equal access to operative cases, these potential young heroines questioned the adequacy of their own training. Women in surgery, in 1980, still faced harsh struggles based on sexism, even for some who were Caucasian.

Was I naïve enough to expect equal access to what was often described as 'a man's world'?

Was it my small size? At only 5 feet 5 inches, one hundred and twenty-five pounds, I was not an imposing physical presence.

Was it the color of my skin? Was it the size of my hands? Was it the lack of a 'Y' chromosome?

Without my preceptor's recommendation, no program would consider me for surgery. I was stubborn. I pressed on with my applications hoping for a good outcome. Limiting my choices to programs within my reach, I waited for Match Day.

When other classmates were celebrating their wonderful new lives, their transitions to new places, I was locked in Dr. Haynes' office, as she made the necessary phone calls to find an opening for a surgical intern.

There was no celebrating for me on Match Day.

Fortunately, Dr. Harold Freeman Chairman of Surgery at Harlem Hospital was willing to accept me in as a surgical intern. A previous stroke of luck had landed me there for my pediatric surgical rotation. I knew their system. I knew Dr. Barlow, Chief of Pediatric Surgery. And, Dr. Barlow was equally kind, intelligent, and fierce.

I had been given a chance to excel and demonstrate my skills in surgery. I again had an opportunity to work with Dr. Barlow and my attraction to pediatric surgery grew stronger. I was grateful for the expected trust that I would excel and complete the residency program.

PAGING DOCTOR SCANTLEBURY

The first time you hear your name being paged, it sends chills down your spine.

I am actually a doctor; Dr. Velma Scantlebury.

It does not stop the countless number of times your name is mispronounced. It does not stop the drain on one's joy taken by those who degrade you, your name and your heritage, out of simple disrespect.

As an intern, the lowest doctor in the traditional hierarchy, you do as you are told.

But still, I was now a doctor. I was clad in tradition, physically and historically.

I still recall 'the ceremony'. There is a room filled with those who survived the rigors of medical school filling scores of auditorium seats. As our names were called, each of us walked to the stage, climbed another set of stairs, and was presented with the 'white coat'. Parents, friends, lovers, and teachers watched a room change from muted grays and browns and blues to brilliant white. A new class of actual doctors was now recognized. I was one. I was glad. The ceremony was humbling.

Now, in the tradition of New York City hospitals, the newly-recognized male doctors would start their new assignments wearing all white: white pants and the hard-earned white jacket. For the females, it was a white skirt and a short white jacket. We were proud, frightened-but-ready, and eager to serve.

I endured the 'scut work'. It ranged from drawing blood to wheeling patients to procedures and picking up X-ray films for the next day operative cases. Such tasks as performing circumcisions on the newborn male babies were reserved for selected interns. Nonetheless, they were surgical procedures, which needed precision and flawlessness. I looked forward to the artful performances.

The only other opportunity to operate as the primary surgeon was in contact with patients seen in the outpatient clinics. Luck was with me one day, as a new patient walked up to the nursing station looking for a doctor. She has just delivered a baby a few weeks before, and was told she had gallstones that needed to be removed. BINGO!

I introduced myself as a surgeon, (she knew nothing of the difference between an intern and a resident) and offered to take care of her needs. It would be my first real case as an intern.

Taunted by my senior residents about the many hours it would take for me to remove her gallbladder, I realized I had to prove them wrong.

With the advice and directions of a chief resident, I was hauled off to the morgue to practice the operation on an unclaimed body. I learned the anatomy, the variations to expect, and the art of dissection. I made myself ready - yet again - beyond what I thought might be required.

The day came for that special surgery. My first cholecystectomy: I was going to remove this lady's gallbladder. My nervousness was obvious: my hands shook as I braced to make the skin incision. As the scalpel made contact to the skin, I found a way to make it glide, smoothly, across her upper right abdomen as I made the standard incision below her right rib cage. As quickly as they came, my tremors disappeared.

Moving through the layers of skin, I entered the abdomen, in the manner I had envisioned. It was real, the diseased gallbladder, laden with stones, within my grasp, ready to be removed. Success was never so exhilarating, for me and my patient.

She was back in the recovery room in less than the predicted four hours. In fact, God had blessed me with an uncomplicated case. She was fully awake by the second hour after a successful surgery; a surgery performed by me.

I was going to be a great surgeon.

The world of surgery was still a man's world. I was still a woman. It required an inner strength to rise above the pack. The quiet demeanor had to be replaced by assertiveness. Act like a man and be assertive and you will be labeled as being too aggressive.

Be nice and be labeled soft, or weak. Medical training did not cover how to handle the novelty of women as surgeons. There is little preparation given on how to deal with the jokes about women from senior staff surgeons. If I refused to laugh, I was said to 'lack a sense of humor'. When inappropriate racial comments were made, I was told I was 'too sensitive'. I had the guidance of the female residents who were farther along in the program and process. I watched the obnoxious behavior directed towards the female surgical residents. Males promoted other males. I would not be belittled. I would not be submissive.

I became aggressive, with a smile. It was determination. It was 'aggressive diplomacy'. I followed the leadership of my female chief resident and allowed my passion for surgery to grow. The hope was for all the endless possibilities to bloom. But I still carried the antacids in my coat pocket.

THE GOOD DOCTOR BARLOW

The vision of being a pediatric surgeon was solidified the first time I met Dr. Barbara Barlow. She was the first female surgical attending I encountered as a medical student at Columbia University, College of Physicians and Surgeons. She was also the Chief of Pediatric Surgery at Harlem Hospital Center in New York City. Her operative skills, calm demeanor, and a tremendously engaging bedside manner was a spectacular combination. I wanted that. I wanted to be seen like that. She sparked the idea that pediatric surgery was where I belonged.

As an intern in general surgery at Harlem Hospital, I gravitated toward pediatric surgery because I was in awe of Dr. Barlow. She operated with finesse, and made any operation seem easy.

She would often walk with, or carry her, patients from the prep area to the operating table. She held their hands or spoke to them softly as they were gently put to sleep. She would describe the bubblegum flavored anesthetic drug that they would inhale as they drifted off to sleep.

She was the first surgeon that I saw use dermabond, the liquid adhesive, on her patients' wounds. We called it surgical glue. She had her special electric, hand-held fan in the OR that she would use to move the air and allow the surgical glue to bond to the skin. There would be no removable sutures used on any of her children. That would be torture to the children.

Dr. Barlow had to be one of the palest White women I knew. Due to her skin condition she avoided direct sunlight, so this made her even paler in appearance. However, she was a force. She was a force with which to be reckoned.

She advocated for her pediatric patients, specifically due to the increasing number of trauma deaths that she saw in Harlem Hospital. These deaths were from children falling out of open windows. She took on politician after politician and eventually won her fight to have landlords install window gates in apartments preventing many more deaths.

Dr Barlow became my mentor and advocated to advance my career as a pediatric surgeon. She made sure I did the maximum number of months allowed on her service. I was taught the fine art of operating on babies and small children. She opened the door to research opportunities. Laboratory research and publications are a necessity for gaining successful pediatric surgical training.

Such an opportunity arose later while completing a rotation in transplant surgery with Dr. Mark Hardy. He was instrumental in starting the Transplant Program at Columbia Presbyterian Hospital. It was my first introduction to transplantation. The ability to restore normal organ function by transplanting a new organ was a phenomenal skill. I observed the many young women and men after surgery, feeling renewed and 'different' as their bodies were now capable of removing the chemicals stored in their systems despite daily dialysis.

Being in the operating room with Dr. Hardy was exhilarating. Whether it was constructing a dialysis fistula or connecting a new kidney, his interests in his patient went beyond the surgical operation. He showed a commitment to his patients and saw them long after they were discharged. His patients loved him.

His heavy accent belied his Polish ancestry. Everyone was greeted with a broad smile and drawn into the big embrace of his broad shoulders - willingly or unwillingly.

While on patient rounds with Dr. Hardy discussions were initiated. These were on subjects such as why transplanted kidneys responded to the drug dopamine after surgery. This medication was used to achieve better urine output. Some topics were in line with why blood vessels were connected but not nerves. The lively talks included debates about how did the kidneys received directives.

Almost always, there would be the interjection; "we should test this in the lab."

This opened up an opportunity for me to do six months of research in his laboratory, resulting in a publication, and setting the stage for my push to a pediatric surgical career.

I was moving closer to my ultimate goal. This was progress. But that was only six months, and it proved insufficient. I learned that my research background was bordering on being inadequate for taking the next step. As I interviewed for pediatric surgery training positions two years ahead of graduation, I knew I needed more time doing research.

It was obvious that another wall needed to be scaled. Despite my dapper appearance, I was no match for the vast number of connected, privileged, white males interviewing as my competitors for a pediatric surgery fellowship.

They all had greater than two years of research experience, and many were applying for the second or third time for fellowship positions. There had never been a Black female pediatric surgery fellow. But others had made it. Dr. James Franklin Densler was the first African-American to practice pediatric surgery in the United States in 1969. With the onset of national regulation of surgical practice, Dr. Samuel Blanton Rosser became the first African-American certified in pediatric surgery in 1975. Others had broken the color barrier. But they were men. Surgery was still a man's world.

My disappointment grew as each interview concluded. Always the only African-American female in the room, ignored by most, the feeling was like having spinach in one's teeth, having others know it, but no one makes you aware of what could improve your chances of acceptance.

At each place the interview was superficial. It was a courtesy, obligatory meeting before the preordained rejection would be delivered.

My interview at Children's Hospital of Pittsburgh with Dr. Mark Ravitch, Professor of Pediatric Surgery, was the best glimmer of hope given. While I did not land a position as a pediatric surgical fellow, I was given a recommendation and a referral to work with Dr. Starzl, the renowned transplant pioneer, for two years as a research fellow. He then suggested that it would then be possible to finish my pediatric fellowship in Pittsburgh.

The missing link was identified. I had to have more training. My previous work in kidney transplant laboratory research had established my interest and would be the launch point for continued work with Dr. Starzl. He would intervene on my behalf. He would be my advocate.

I left Pittsburgh, and my interview, with a new hope. A new opportunity was visible. A path was being created by one surgeon (who knew little about me) because he, perhaps, saw my determination and opened that door to other possibilities.

This was a clear case of continuing to try to see the other side (of the wall).

More confident than ever, the excitement about leaving New York for the next stage of my career grew in the months ahead. I stayed focused, and completed my chief residency with little fanfare. God is good.

MEETING THE MASTER SURGEON - STARZL

The journey was beginning. I would later return to Pittsburgh for a lengthy stay. But this time the purpose was for my interview with Dr. Starzl. His office was on a lower level and I sat outside waiting for his return and my interview.

Dr. Mann, a junior attending, walked in and immediately assumed I was Dr. Starzl's wife. I could only assume that she was young and Black.

Dr. Starzl soon appeared, and first verified who I was and why I was there.

He stated, "Well, if Mark said I should take you on as a fellow, then, by gosh, that's what I am going to do."

Off we went to lunch. With strides much greater than mine, I struggled to keep up as my three-inch heeled shoes and skirt suit limited the size and quickness of my steps. I resorted to a run-walk mode, hoping he would not notice my forced, distracting conversation.

The doctors' cafeteria was across a hallway from the recovery room on the 2nd floor of the hospital. Grabbing one tray, Dr. Starzl selected two Shasta diet drinks, one serving of green peas, and one chicken breast, along with one extra plate. He also picked up two sets of utensils.

We approached the cashier.

"Put this on my tab.", he said to the cashier.

"Oh no, you don't. You have not paid your bill in months. No further credit. You have to pay in cash." That was the surprising response from the cashier.

Dr. Starzl simply said, "I don't have any cash on me." While patting his pockets first at the chest level of his blue doctor's coat, then the side pockets of his pants he seemed to resolve that he would have no success in satisfying the cashier. They were equals. He was holding less power.

The cashier was firm, "Too bad, you have to pay today."

I offered to pay for the meal, which was OK with me. There was little choice at the time. I was paying for lunch at my own interview. This was going to be memorable.

Dr. Starzl proceeded to divide the peas into 2 portions, split the chicken breast into two pieces and we each had our own drink. Was I imagining the fact that he actually counted the number of peas?

I was in awe of being with a master surgeon of such repute. The rest of the situation was beyond bemusement. With all that swirling, I cannot remember the cost of the meal.

We sat down and talked for a while about life matters. It was a personal talk, an interview about me - not just my skills and resume.

After the interview ended, I headed back to the main entrance. As I made my way back along a hallway, checking to make sure no one was in sight, I jumped up to see if I could click my heels like Dorothy in the Wizard of Oz. I could not imagine how easy that went.

I was to be back in Pittsburgh in another year.

PITTSBURGH

Pittsburgh was viewed as a city of steel mills and smoke stacks, but not for anything in medicine other than a place for training. That is what I thought as I approached the city for my transplant fellowship training.

The drive from New York City was long and arduous, miles of green pastures, rolling hills and short tunnels. There were cows, cows, and more cows to view as interstate I-76 wound its way across the vast plains of Pennsylvania.

After unloading my items into the new apartment, my sister and I took a walk around the neighborhood. People we did not know spoke to us, smiled and were polite.

"Do they know you already?, she asked.

"No. I guess they are just nice folks here."

The new introduction to Pittsburgh was not without drama.

PITTSBURGH - Night One

Before the evening was over, I succumbed to bleeding from the space left behind from the removal of the last of my wisdom teeth. It had been removed only 2 days earlier. I tried to stop it, and failed, with all the recommended family remedies. We headed to the emergency room.

After waiting more than 5 hours, the bleeding was remedied by one simple solution: bite on a unused tea bag. It worked.

I returned home to an uneventful evening to prepare for the next day. Since I was unemployed at the time of my emergency room visit, I had to pay the cost of medical care and the price of a tea bag.

Fifteen hundred dollars. It was an expensive tea bag

As the night passed, there was a difference to the sounds or lack thereof.

Without the noise of sirens, and police cars, we concentrated on the birds chirping outside the window. We were definitely not in New York City. It would take time to get used to Pittsburgh's relatively quiet nights.

Over the next week, there were no initial exciting revelations. There was a series of steps required in the hiring process. I had to learn, and adhere to, regulations for gaining access to the proper buildings, to patient data, and to the operating rooms.

I would be here for 2 years to complete a research fellowship. Yes, I hoped to be in the operating room on occasion, but my short-term goal would not be overshadowed - I had to be a pediatric surgeon. I would follow in Dr. Barlow's footsteps.

Once all the paperwork was completed, I was put to work immediately. I was sent into a room where Dr. Newell was doing a kidney transplant. As I walked in he was in a corner of the operating room working on dissecting and preparing the kidney.

The patient was already asleep on the table. This was a young adult. It was my first working introduction to Dr. Newell, and to kidney transplantation at Children's Hospital of Pittsburgh.

Dr. Newell asked, "Have you done a kidney transplant before?"

"Yes sir." I replied.

I failed to mention that mine was peripheral involvement, and that it was at least three years ago.

"OK, then go ahead and get started on the patient. We'll put in the kidney from the right side. Make the incision and start the operation,", Dr. Newell instructed.

At this point, I thought that those were a very long three years ago. I definitely thought that I had gotten myself into deep horse manure.

Slowly, I began to prep the patient after shaving the area for surgery. In my mind the thoughts were that I needed to quickly recall how Dr. Hardy performed his kidney transplants, those three years ago that seemed like eons.

In my laser-focused efforts to get to Pittsburgh and this point, I failed to prepare myself for the moment when I would have to perform. This was the moment, and, I could not fail.

The room was warm, and the patient was undressed. I prepared the area for surgery and placed the necessary catheter in the bladder to monitor urine made from the new kidney.

Thank God I remembered this step.

I scrubbed, gowned and readied the patient slowly. I was trying to buy time and recall the various steps in the successful procedure I saw performed earlier and to emulate it.

I made the incision, nervously.

"Curve from the hip area to the midline region above the bikini line.

Good. Down through the fat layers, muscle and fascia, then muscle again."

All was going well. I needed help with retraction and the scrub nurse assistant offered it. Within minutes, an experienced visiting surgeon came to the table to offer his assistance.

He had done this before, obviously many times. He literally exposed the areas, and marked the direction I should take. He saved me from much embarrassment.

Finally, Dr. Newell came to the table and, without a beat, continued the surgery. The tried-and-true practice, the philosophy of 'see one, do one, teach one' was in full effect. It was to my benefit.

I had performed my first kidney transplant not totally, but this is the way I saw it. I made the skin incision, dissected down to the patient's artery and vein, and was given an opportunity to connect the vein portion on my side of the operation. With the blood released into the new kidney, the awakening of the organ was dramatic. The color changed from grayish-brown to pink; in this context, pink is the beginning of success.

As the kidney received the new blood, it began to function immediately. It was exhilarating to witness clear liquid squirting out into the wound.

"Don't worry" said Dr. Dr. Newell.

"It's all sterile. No bugs. Just clean pee."

FELLOWSHIP YEARS

Some of us were slated to do research, primarily, and others would have clinical responsibilities. With vast numbers of donor operations and transplant surgeries to perform, research was given less of a priority for those licensed to practice medicine and surgery. Pittsburgh was the 'Mecca' for liver transplantation at the time.

Patients were referred from across the country, and our practice grew to over five hundred liver transplants and nearly four hundred kidney transplant annually, in both adults and children.

As ten fellows in training, we filled the void of physicians needing to care for the adult liver and kidney services, the pediatric liver and kidney operations, as well as accompanying those more qualified to recover organs donated from deceased patients from all across the country.

Long stretches of donor 'runs' kept us away from home and the comforts of long hot showers. The trophies collected were the various hues of operating scrub clothes that we wore, in the rush to exit the donor hospital.

Thanks to the nursing staff, we were reminded of our heightened body odor.

There were occasions when several teams would arrive at our operating rooms in Pittsburgh at nearly the same time. This led to there being a stack of three or four kidneys along with two livers waiting to be implanted.

All that was required during those days was a visual confirmation that your assigned liver for patient A was not confused with a different liver chosen for patient B. If both livers were from donors with the same blood type, then only size mattered. Liver transplantation required the patient and donor to be compatible by blood type, and that it can fit into the space left behind by removal of the old diseased liver.

After the organs for use were placed in the designated patient's operating room, the back table procedure or 'cleaning up' of the organ (removal of unnecessary tissues and fat, as well as preparing the vein and arteries for connection) were completed by the senior fellows, or more experienced visiting surgeons. First year fellows were often assistants on donor organ retrievals and upon their return, assisted on recipient operations. There was little time to rest.

This was the routine for us during our first year of fellowship. Our office spaces were equipped with long pillowed couches, as there was little time to sleep at home. The best naps came during long "donor runs" to retrieve organs for implantation. The further away the donor, the greater opportunity to sleep.

Long flights were accompanied by meals for our return trips home, perhaps a seafood platter or a sandwich tray. The blissful rest and replenishments, provided without reachable access by phone or beeper, was a privilege to be appreciated. Such a benefit would be short-lived pleasure ended by an organ that failed to function immediately or required replacement within days.

There were consequences to failure. As a first-year fellow, you were overshadowed by the second-year fellow, or the skillful visiting surgeon who already mastered the art of the donor operation. A liver that failed to function had to be replaced urgently.

Was the poor quality of the liver not recognized by the accepting surgeon?

Did the donor surgeon take too long to remove the liver to be transplanted?

Was the warm blood removed and the organ cooled to a low temperature in a swift fashion?

The blame had to fall on someone. That someone would be handed a 'hiatus' from donor surgeries, until privileges were granted again. It was "the way" in Pittsburgh.

It was the price to pay.

OPERATIONS

Seemingly, there were scores of bodies in the room. They should have raised the temperature, but did not. It was cold, and stark. Even the room seemed to have an attitude - a serious one.

The clot of surgeons moving about were changing shifts. It was a long, difficult case.

Dr. Starzl had taken a break and was back. Many units of blood were required for this young child who was barely staying alive as the great surgeons worked to get her scarred liver out.

Dr. Starzl relieved Dr. Yang, another attending, started working again. Everyone standing was tense. A life was in the balance and exhalations from nurses, technicians, and the surgeons were bright sounds in a dampened room.

The patient's blood vessels were requisitely tiny for her age and condition. Dr. Starzl was wearing magnifying loops to do the necessary differentiations perfectly. There were four surgeons at the table, all hands in the small open abdomen. The suctions were rhythmic, removing excess blood from the field.

"Move your hands, for heaven's sake; I can't see a damn thing!", said Dr. Starzl.

One or two surgeons withdrew their hands from retracting duties, not knowing whose hands he wanted moved.

"I still can't see, damn it!" Dr. Starzl exclaimed.

There were no hands left in the field, except his, at this point.

He continued, "Damn it! I said move your hands!"

With that said, he picked up an instrument and hit the remaining hand he could see in his field of vision. The hand was his own.

We all kept silent, leaving the air open for his next words.

FLIGHT LEADER

Dr. Starzl occasionally did a donor recovery while I was a first year fellow. Early one morning, we were headed to Wisconsin to recover the liver as all other surgeons were either doing cases or out recovering other organs. This was a pediatric case.

Dr. Starzl was peculiar about who recovers the pediatric organs and so off we went with one of the Japanese visiting surgeons. It was winter. Cold, he was bundled in a green down coat, and we settled in on the jet. Dr. Starzl went off to sleep.

Halfway there he awoke, startled, and stated, "Dog-gonnit, I have to get this paper corrected and off to the editor tonight before FedEx closes. How soon can we get back?"

We were given a six-hour maximum turnaround time from wheels-up. Working furiously, he pulled out his manuscript and began editing.

"Any coffee on board?", he asked in something just short of a demand.

Handed some warm version of the intended beverage, he gulped a mouth full only to remark, "Shoot! This is worse than drinking engine oil!"

He slapped his thighs, teased and prodded the jet's co-pilot that taking off as soon as possible was the only acceptable outcome. Having instructed the pickup team that we were in need of an ambulance or police escort, he aimed to minimize time on the ground. Dr. Starzl demanded it. He also, demanded that the patient be in the operating room at time of our arrival.

Whisked from the airport, and escorted by ambulance and police to the donor hospital, we arrived in time to be met by his surgical colleague from the area. Taken to the surgical lounge to change into clean scrubs, I was left standing, seeking a female nurse to guide me to the nurses' locker room to change.

Unable to find a female to give me access to clean scrubs, Dr. Starzl takes me into the male locker room, tells me to select a larger size, which was placed over my current scrubs.

Off we went to the assigned operating room, to proceed with the recovery, in an expeditious manner.

Blue lights - again. Dr. Starzl quickly opened the abdomen, placed a perfusion cannula in the main blood vessel of the body and, with another positioned below the heart, he was ready in less than ten minutes to remove the liver.

If it were some Twilight Zone episode (in Wisconsin), the tick-tock, the gong of a pendulum would be sounding out of view. We all heard our own heartbeats, and imagined sensing the move of each second hand traversing our watches.

The donor was given heparin to prevent clotting; then came the rapid clamping and flushing of the entirety of the abdominal organ set with cold preservative fluid.

The liver turned from red to a dull light brown color. We watched as the intestines also drained of blood which was now all emptying through a large opening in the heart into the chest cavity. There was, still, the clock and the clocks in our heads, and the blue light, and the cold air, and the shared knowledge of our mission. Our thoughts were heavy yet serene. The room was full of breathing and gurgling and muffled grunts.

Once the liver was cooled, with ice placed around the vital organs, care was then taken to quickly remove it. With the absence of blood, I could not tell artery from vein, or from lymphatic structures. But, I watched as his hands made the scissors glide around the vital structures, and carefully preserved the important attachments that were needed for implanting the liver at our destination.

It was certainly a case of snatch and run.

Within an hour of having entered the operating room we were on our way out. Even without removing our scrub clothes, the liver was packed on ice and off we were by ambulance, escorted by police and sirens to the county airport to meet our Learjet.

With deadlines to meet, Dr. Starzl continued to work on his manuscript on the ride home. Once picked up by the driver back in Pittsburgh it was off to his office to complete the next task. This was indeed the most rapid of all rapid recoveries in which I ever participated. This would be the way Pittsburgh trained surgeons would be known to recover organs for transplant.

It was surgical training, it was hero training, it was what will forever make Pittsburgh - Starzl-trained fellows and surgeons different.

It was the Starzl way.

LAUGHING - MATTERS

Peter and I were asked to assist Dr. Starzl on an adult kidney transplant case. Peter, American born of Japanese descent, was from California and acted like it. His demeanor was more relaxed than the rest of us, and he walked the hallways with his head down, shaking it from side to side. I was never sure if he was conveying the message: 'I can't believe what is taking place', or the thought of 'what an incredible place this is!'

Another surgeon arrived, ahead of the team and Dr. Starzl, and was working on preparing the kidney by removing the extra fat from around the kidney and isolating the blood vessels that would be used for connecting the donor kidney in the patient.

We quickly scrubbed into the case before Dr. Starzl arrived.

Once the kidney was brought up to the opened incision, Dr. Starzl began to connect patient's blood vessels to the blood vessels of the kidney. As fellows, with experience in watching and doing, we both noticed that the kidney was not oriented correctly. The lower half of the kidney contains the structure that allows urine to drain from the kidney. This tube-like structure also needs to be connected to the patient's urine bladder, so that the urine made from the kidney will pass right into the bladder. This lower end of the kidney should be positioned towards the feet of the patient. Instead, the kidney was being connected with the lower end towards the patient's head.

With our eyes and head communicating, Peter and I dared each other to say something. Finally, Peter began.

"Ehhh, Dr. Starzl, can I say something?" His voice was muffled behind the blue paper masks we all wore.

Dr. Starzl snapped back, "No. Just be quiet and shut up!"

"OK Dr. Starzl.", Peter had gone as far as was wise, if not beyond.

Peter glared at me over the round-framed glasses that sat on the edge of his nose. He shook his head and raised his eyebrows along with his shoulders, as if to say 'well, I tried'.

As one side of the first blood vessel was connected, we moved to the next. Peter motioned to me, with a tilt of his head and eyes pointed towards Dr. Starzl, he hinted that it was now up to me to speak up.

I cleared my throat a few times and nervously attempted to get the words out of my mouth. But with the quiet tone of my voice, behind the thick multi-layered surgical mask, projected only a muffled accumulation of garbled sounds.

Dr. Starzl thought I was voicing my displeasure at being asked to assist.

"Do you not want to be here? Is there someplace you would rather be?" he snapped.

I responded, "No Sir, I am happy to be here. This is where I want to be!"

Dr. Starzl continued with the blood vessel connections. Peter looked at me beneath furrowed eyebrows. I had failed in expressing the issue. Peter was not giving up.

He attempted, again, to warn Dr. Starzl about the orientation of the kidney.

Peter said, "Dr. Starzl, there is something I need to tell you."

Dr. Starzl, "Didn't I say to be quiet?" (this is the 'de-salted' language version) Peter went on, "But, Dr. Starzl..."

Dr. Starzl let loose, "This is a critical moment- wait until I am finished."

Peter had no choice but to respond with, "If you say so, Sir."

The anastomoses completed, clamps were removed, and the kidney was unwrapped from the white lap pad, only to reveal that the lower pole of the kidney is now in the upper position. Words cannot describe the tirade that ensued.

Dr. Starzl shouted at the room, "Why the hell did you not say something earlier? You both stood here and did not utter a meaningful (clean version) word!!!"

Peter managed to get a few words in, with, "I was trying to tell you, Sir, but you insisted I shut up!"

With that, Dr. Starzl left the case to be completed by another attending. We were both going to be in the doghouse for a few days. The patient did well as the urinary drainage tube was connected to the patient in a different way, but successful nonetheless.

TABATHA - A SHORT SUCCESS

Saving a life was worth going against the grain for Dr. Starzl. He was unconventional in his way of thinking, but that made him who he was. His success in being a pioneer in liver transplantation came with the price of failure. Many lives were lost before he was able to have the first successful liver transplant. In 1987, his thoughts were likely along the same path. Always learn, then take another step forward.

Born in Madisonville, Kentucky, Tabatha suffered a twisted small intestine at birth, resulting in a condition called short-gut syndrome. Suffering damage to ninety-five percent of her small bowel, it was removed two days after birth. Unable to eat, she survived on highly concentrated intravenous feedings until age 3. Sadly, such feedings injured her liver, resulting in liver failure.

Given only a few weeks to live, Tabatha and her mother arrived in Pittsburgh hoping for a liver transplant. A replaced liver would only be subject to the same damage, unless her small intestine was replaced.

Immediately, Dr. Starzl proposed not just replacing her liver and intestine, but much more. With all the scar tissue in her abdomen, removing her organs, en masse, would allow for an easier surgery, technically, but, it brought more complications for the immune system to handle.

The proposed multi-organ transplant would consist of 5 organs all connected: the liver, small intestine, pancreas and parts of the stomach and colon. The operation took 15 hours, and was the third such operation performed in this country.

Such an operation was first performed by Dr. Starzl at Children's hospital in 1983, and the second at Rush-Presbyterian Hospital in early 1987. Both patients died after a few days. Knowing the challenges that they were about to face were enormous, only the senior surgeons were part of the donor and recipient teams.

The donor organs were flown from Virginia, from an infant declared brain dead after a tragic motor vehicle accident. Tabitha was the first patient to survive for more than a few days. She cleared her 6 month milestone and was known to all the staff and physicians at Children's Hospital of Pittsburgh.

No one dared write orders on Tabatha without first clearing them with Dr. Tzakis and Dr. Starzl. They would appear any time, day or night, to check on her progress. Each day, a stream of visiting surgeons trailed after Dr. Starzl, mesmerized by the chubby-cheeked 3 year old who made her presence known to all the staff. Whether it was a tantrum thrown when her demands were not met, or a refusal to eat or try different foods, Tabatha was known for her feistiness and unwillingness to yield to the doctors. She would often be found sitting in the nurses' station rather than hanging out in the playroom. She was fond of the chairs because they spun around. She was sent many gifts from across the country. She embraced them.

Tabatha's course was complicated by chronic issues with her liver. The balancing act of preventing rejection, by using many drugs, resulted in a weakening of her body. She eventually died of a blood infection that shut down her major organs and eventually her heart. That was just 6 months after her landmark surgery.

Her life touched many, including President Ronald Reagan who made a public statement in his weekly radio address, asking the public to pray for her. In the news conference following her death, Dr. Starzl was moved to tears, and commented about the willingness of her parents to give her a chance at living, knowing her original liver had failed. She lived 6 months, but died before her 4th birthday.

LEARNING THE TRADE

Among our duties as first-year fellows was carrying out 'donor runs' with the visiting surgeons. We traveled across the country, Tennessee, South Carolina, and even California, to retrieve viable organs to transplant into anxiously waiting recipients.

Eager to start liver transplant surgery in their own countries, several well skilled surgeons from various locations in South America would take the lead. Whether it was Dr. Cardina, an Argentine surgeon with a soft voice and calm demeanor, or Dr. Rodriguez, visiting from San Paulo, Brazil, the dissections of deceased donors was a skill that could be learned from those willing to teach.

On one such trip, we arrived in California for a young pediatric donor. The child had been declared brain dead (no measurable blood flow to the brain) by state regulations. As the child was being transferred to the operative table, spontaneous leg switches were noted on the left leg. An alarmed nurse immediately questioned the documentation of brain dead and halted the procedure. Repeated neurological examinations, and further delays cause Dr. Cardina to question using this young child as a donor.

One call was made to Dr. Starzl to gain his opinion. The decision was clearly established by his short conversation. An audible, but muffled, voice emanated from the phone, held away from Dr. Cardina's ear while he worked to verbalize his repeated "Yes, Sir" responses.

With the appropriate expert medical confirmation, that these 'abnormal movements' can be seen even after the brain dies, we proceeded, silently, with the removal of the liver for donation.

It was difficult to ignore the repetitive movements during the operation. As uncomfortable as we were, as the organ retrieval team, we could only imagine how alarming it had been to other staff and even family. The medical specialist stayed behind to give further explanation to the team and the nurses. This patient had no ability to breath on their own because there were no brain signals being sent out, but somehow the nerves to the muscles that cause movement were spontaneously firing on their own! How bizarre was that?!

A new lesson was learned that day. It was unforgettable, but clearly to be encountered again and again.

That experience stayed with me for many years. I still experience the uncertainty that each of us shared as we traveled back from California. No one spoke. It was a long 5 hours home.

Over the next few years, I accumulated similar memories of different donor surgeries that would remain lodged in my brain; they refused to be dislodged.

Whether performing surgery on a pregnant mother who lost her life, or on the aspiring football player impaled by a truck while riding his motorcycle, I had to focus on the lives to be saved by the gifts donated because of loving families.

Donor surgeries were unlike anything we practiced during surgical residency training. Those were about removing diseased gallbladders, or cancers from colons, or repairing injuries from gunshot wounds. These patients underwent surgery to improve or save their lives.

That was what made transplanting organs unique. It is using that which can no longer be beneficial at death to help save the life of another.

As I became efficient in my skills as a transplant donor surgeon, I took on the role of lead surgeon. On many occasions, the racial and gender biases of many Caucasian surgeons, especially in the southern states, were evident as soon as I entered the room. Women of color, as general surgeons, were less than 1% of the number of licensed and trained surgeons, especially in the south. Women in sub-specialties were an even smaller number of the whole, regardless of color. When I walked into an operating room, I was assumed to be anything other than the transplant surgeon.

The conversation would begin by the heart surgeon introducing himself to the male Caucasian transplant coordinator. To them, the white male had to be the one in charge.

The transplant coordinator, would often play along, only to let them know at the end of their 'this is what I will be doing' speech, that, "This is Dr. Scantlebury, she will be the lead surgeon." He would then correct them, much to their inevitable chagrin, announcing that he was only the coordinator.

Remarkably the annoyance and disdain were so obvious that they would often refuse to respect my presence or acknowledge that I could possibly be the surgeon leading the team.

Then it happened. On one donor run the cardiac surgeon was a female. That was a great moment for me. She was very professional, respectful and skillful. She proceeded to dissect the areas around the heart, and without much time wasted, quickly clamped the necessary structures. With expert movements, she cut the blood vessels to allow drainage of warm blood and immediately cooled the heart down with sterile ice placed all around its perimeter.

Watching that donor heart slowly decrease in heart rate, fluttering and then stopping completely was remarkable. Quickly she removed the vital organ, transferred it to a container with more ice and saline, wrapped it up and was out the door. She thanked everyone for his or her assistance and took off. We were left uncertain if that heart was to be transplanted or it used for research. I was humbled to be at the table with her. Not all cardiac surgeons were men.

She had broken down a wall of her own and had claimed her right to be at the table. I watched as she exited the room, with grace and confidence. I wished to do the same. I finished my recovery of the liver and kidneys, and returned home reflecting on what had just transpired.

I could now stand taller, both for her and for me.

'REAL DOCTOR'

"When is the real doctor coming to see me?"

This was said more than once, in multiple places, throughout the U.S.

This patient, despite receiving a successful liver transplant by me refused to accept the fact that I was her surgeon: the one who performed her operation. I saw her each day after her surgery, introducing myself each time, and for a rare occasion, actually wore my white coat, indicating I was a surgeon. Her mind evidently refused to process what she was being told and what she was actually seeing. She was thankful for the success of the operation. Always though, it was because of "the great work being done" at this Pittsburgh hospital; nothing was about me.

Often it required a certain level of restraint to bite my tongue, but while my mind had a different response, my outward action was one of calm.

Often, I had to enlighten Caucasian patients about my credentials, accomplishments, and leadership experiences. The wall they erected was one that assumed I could not be Black - AND - a 'real doctor' at the same time. There was also the expectation that if I could look over their walls on those two points, that I could not add 'woman' to the mix.

They were patients. I extended their lives. Their prejudices regarding my sex, race, and attained position - somehow - overshadowed how intimately we were recently involved.

When my hands were inside of those Caucasian bodies, I saw nothing but a patient needing my help. I saw what I could do with a lovingly given organ to prolong a life. I did it, always, with care and without thought to the skin that would be closed over my work when the transplant was complete.

"Was the organ from a male or female?" This was a familiar question.

"Was the donor Black or White?" Some patients wanted to know.

I would explain that when a donor becomes available, we consider size, blood results and how well the organ is functioning. Beyond the outside skin, all persons look the same on the inside. There was blood, yellow fat, a heart, two lungs, a liver and often two kidneys. Inside was all the same despite the outer skin hues of yellow, brown, taupe or black.

I am, indeed the real doctor. Whether it was my youthful appearance or the color of my skin that made these patient encounters so bizarre, was uncertain. I do know that the other physicians I worked with did not encounter the same resistance.

As surgical fellows we spent nearly all our days in scrub wear. Usually, the colorful ones we failed to leave behind upon leaving the last hospital where we had done a donor recovery. Our uniforms could confuse outsiders - especially ones who had closed minds about what our roles must have been.

The white coats, from our 'transformation' ceremony day were rarely worn. In the actual work environment, it was a revolving door in, and out, of the operating room. It was noble, humbling, frightening, and it was work.

Very often, patients were more likely to believe that I was there to empty the bed pan, pick up their meal trays or empty their garbage.

It was Pittsburgh. It was 1988. It was a far cry from Harlem Hospital in New York. Despite being a city of twelve percent minority residents, there were few physicians of color. Rather than feeling like 'Dorothy', in the Wizard of Oz, as I did after my initial interview, I now felt like "The Little Engine that Could". I could not allow the negative perceptions to cause me to lose my self-esteem and my hope for my future.

Almost routinely, it required a deep fortitude from within my core to not be offended by the patients or staff who failed to accept my capabilities because of my skin hue.

I had to remain focused. Yes, the work was long and arduous. But my gratification came from the wonderful patients who were grateful for having a new opportunity to enjoy life.

Most patients had only encountered Caucasian surgeons. They came to expect this. Women were expected to have different roles; as recommended for me as a medical student.

"Consider dermatology." I was advised back then.

One patient used his religious beliefs as an excuse for his behavior. No woman could see his naked body.

Another questioned, "Are you sure you know what you are doing? Should you not call someone else to help you?"

The wall of rejection could sometimes be held up by my own surgical colleagues.

It happened in the early morning hours. A senior attending was called in to do a kidney transplant.

While we were scrubbing our hands at the sink before entering the operating room, he remarked, "Why are you doing this? You should be at home having babies and taking care of your family! This is not a place for a young lady like you!"

Was I not entitled to practice my skills and do the same job as a man?

He was not expecting an answer and I was not in a position to give him one. He left the sink area and proceeded into the room to gown-up for the surgery. It was five in the morning, and he was likely not too pleased about having to come in for a transplant.

As we proceeded to do the surgery, he continued his banter about women in surgery. It was too challenging and stressful for women, he remarked.

His daughter, who was in medical school, was even considering such an 'insane career'.

"I would never understand why you women do this."

No, he did not. And he never will. I kept silent.

He was different.

PUSHING AGAINST THE WALL

On one occasion, I was called to do a liver transplant by one of the senior attendings, Dr. Han, who was Dr. Starzl's right-hand man. His specialty was liver resections for patients with liver cancer. On this day, he was to operate on the liver of an affluent, Jewish stockbroker with known cancer.

Unfortunately, the liver cancer was found to be in many places, making it impossible to remove it all. Instead, the surgery was abandoned and Dr. Han opted to investigate the alternative of replacing his entire liver with a new liver transplant.

Once he was able to get the patient listed and find a liver from a matching donor with the same blood type and body size, he called me to accompany him to discuss the liver transplant procedure with the patient and his family.

Dr. Han walked into the patient's room, and began with, "I have good news and bad news."

"The liver is consumed by a great deal of tumor. It cannot be removed. Good news - we can give you a new liver."

With that, he pointed to me, "This is Dr. Velma. She will do the liver transplant today."

There was obviously information overload. The idea of getting a transplant with no previous understanding of the risks and potential good and bad outcomes was overwhelming.

The shock of being faced with some unknown surgeon taking on such a life-saving operation on their loved one was unnerving. At least this could be discerned by their hesitation, and the look of disbelief on all faces. Their objections were raised, and overturned. Dr. Han stood his ground. He expressed his confidence in me as his pupil.

A request was made, immediately, for private a discussion with Dr. Han. I left the room, and waited outside. Discussion ended and Dr. Han walked out the room.

All that Dr. Han said was, "You do surgery. Let's go set up." And, off we went.

I was assisted by Dr. S, a junior attending. All went well but the liver failed to function immediately. There was the 'tick-tock', the pounding of our own, counted, heartbeats. Again, it was the 'operating theatre'. I had rehearsed my role, established, in my head, the steps that would be taken along the way. I had the skill, and I had been taught - well.

I began the operation. Step-by-step, I recalled how the journey should have proceeded. The methodical nature of how I had been taught would certainly prevent forgetting a vital move. Everything was going smoothly. And, the new liver was sewn in successfully.

I watched as the new liver filled with the patient's blood and regained its pinkish-red color. The area around the new vessel connections was packed with lap pads and we took a quick break to stretch our legs.

Upon our return, we redressed and quickly removed the cotton pads to see how the liver was performing.

The liver produced no bile immediately. It produced only a pale, thin imitation of the real thing. The pounding of the surgical teams' hearts and our teams sweat increased. Even the echoing sound of falling titanium forceps against the tiled floor was rock-&-roll loud, unpleasant, and a mirror of what everyone in the theatre heard - except the patient. I was disappointed, and so were the team members. Efforts to predict the slim possibility of better function were met with resistance and little hope.

We closed the patient and sent him to the ICU. While the general discussion was that things might turn around in the next 24 hours and he should be "just fine", I later sat down with the family and voiced my concern. I needed to be honest, given my junior status. I could be wrong. I would rather be wrong.

Unfortunately, the liver needed to be replaced within 48 hours and we were successful in doing so. He survived and did well for many years. His family gained respect for me and eventually would embrace me as a friend.

Long after his death, from recurrent cancer in the transplanted liver, my relationship with his wife persisted for years to come.

I often pondered what my fate would have been, had I not followed by inner voice and opted for honesty. Observing previous encounters and discussions regarding of transplanted livers that worked poorly or needed immediate replacement were valuable lessons well learned.

JOHN WAYNE (ANOTHER ONE) - MATTERS

He was a country boy from the outskirts of Erie Pennsylvania. There were hundreds of patients listed for kidney transplant. There were no regulations regarding contact with patients added to the listing. They often did not see us until time for the actual surgery.

It was 1988, and Mr. Wayne was admitted for a kidney transplant and I happened to be on call. Entering the room to introduce myself to the patient, he looked at me with shock.

John said, "Are you a doctor?"

My response was, "Yes I am. I will be your surgeon for this operation."

"Oh my God. I have never met a 'real' female doctor, ever. And you are Black too! I actually never met a Black person before. I have seen some Black people, but never really knew any.", he spouted.

I was just as quick in my response, "Yes. Indeed, I am Black. Have been all my life, and the last time I checked (looking at my skin)."

As we wheeled the patient from his room and into the operating room, before we could even get fully into the operating room, he raised up, looked around the room and saw that the entire staff was female: nurses, technicians, anesthesiologists and doctors. He grabbed my hand, as I stood on the other side of the bed rails.

John said, "Please don't kill me. I have a little girl at home that I need to take care of. Oh, please don't kill me. I want to live."

Politely, and quietly, I told him, "John, I have no intentions of letting you die during this operation. With God's help you will wake up and do well. I also have two little girls, and have no plans on going to jail and leaving them behind."

What I wanted to say was, 'I really don't know you from Adam, and have no intentions of taking your life. I am good at what I do, and would you be asking me this question if I was a white male?'

As if reading my thoughts, he stated: "I hope you know what you are doing!"

By this time we had gotten him to the operating table and were positioning him as best as we could. The response to his statement came from the anesthesiologist who reassured him that he had the greatest possible team of "women". She went on to assure him that, when he awoke, he would have had a successful transplant.

John did well, but needed dialysis for one day after his transplant. He later explained that many of his statements were attributable to his nervousness and unfamiliarity with people of color.

As he would return for his clinic visits, I would joke with him and introduce him to as many other Black staff persons as possible. Gradually, he got comfortable, and expressed that he was grateful for the success of a team with so many women of color. He continued to be an advocate for us, referring other patients for transplantation.

ROBBIE - MATTERED

Robbie was eight years old, and needed another kidney transplant. His first, new kidney had been donated by his Dad six years before. It was lost to rejection, so, he was up for another kidney.

Robbie had developed into a very mischievous young man. He was a constant challenge to his parents, and the staff. Then, life and the system challenged Robbie.

He was brought into the hospital because we were notified that there was a matched organ for him. He was told not to eat before his operation. He kept sneaking food in the hours before going to the operating room.

I had to speak up.

"Robbie, you are going to have to be a good boy and try not to eat anymore. It may prevent you from getting this kidney. Could you please listen to us?"

"What if I don't listen?" Robbie asked.

"Well, we might have to do your operation with you awake!" That got his attention.

Robbie surprised me by saying, "I don't care. Put it anywhere." I had to go bigger with this child. So, I said, "I could connect it to the blood vessels in your armpit, and allow the urine to drain through your nipple. Then, every time you squeeze the kidney in your armpit, the urine can squirt out your nipple in the front!"

Robbie said, "NO! Please don't do that! I'll be good!"

Robbie kept his promise and got his transplant. It worked immediately. Before he was ready to go home, he had many questions including, 'what was the sex of his donor?'.

I told him, "Your kidney came from young lady who wanted all her organs to be given to those in need, like you."

Then there was Robbie's next question. He asked, "Does that mean that I will have to sit down to pee?"

SINGLE IN PITTSBURGH

When I imagined my life as an adult, it was one of being in charge of my own practice, making my own schedule and taking care of my patients. I could envision my office and my success. Our mother doted over her new grandchildren, elated to share her love with them. One by one, my siblings were married, increasing the numbers of nieces and nephews around us.

I would constantly remind her, "don't expect any from me, as I plan on being a career woman." With this as an excuse, I could avoid meeting young men and particularly the dating game.

Just about every young lady imagines herself meeting Mr. Right, falling in love and getting married. My 'career woman' excuse justified my lack of focus on dating, but did not entirely dissuade one suitor who was persistent- even though I relegated him to the 'friend zone'. Finishing college and medical school created distance that proved detrimental to the relationship.

I remained focused and despite several good and bad experiences during my five years as a general surgery resident, my further training in transplantation research demanded my focus. Deep within me, I was still looking for Mr. Right, and any attempts to create him from Mr. Wrong were futile efforts. I left it all behind and headed to Pittsburgh.

There were ten fellows hired that year in 1986. There were three females in the group. The other two were married. Both were Caucasian, but so were nearly all the males, except two who were of Japanese origin.

Life in Pittsburgh was busy. It was also lonely. There were gatherings for dinner in various places, and 'fellows' night out after a long week, including many of the visiting surgeons and physicians.

The get-togethers were pleasant enough, but, did not result in any deep friendships with anyone, or even a superficial relationship with either of the two females in the fellowship program.

I found it easier to connect socially with the nurses, particularly those at Children's Hospital and later those on the adult transplant services.

I will always remember Debbie, and Holly in particular. With every award or recognition, I would be reminded by them to start my 'thank you' speech with the statement, "Had it not been for Debbie and Holly I would not be here today." Assuring them I would honor them in this way, I failed to follow through on my promise. But now I have. They will always have a special place in my heart.

Dr. Pascal a pediatric surgeon from Venezuela interested in pediatric liver transplantation, joined our team to learn the fine art of these life-saving surgeries. We shared similar interests, and she became a consistent assistant on nearly all my donor and recipient surgeries.

Life outside of fellowship was non-existent. Essentially there were few, to no, African-American physicians or professionals in my limited social orbit at the time.

Coerced into joining a dating service, I added my profile to one of the online services and, after four 4 months, finally got a potential match. I arranged to meet in a nearby Pittsburgh restaurant for an early afternoon dinner. I waited outside the establishment looking for a person meeting the description given.

As I looked down the sidewalk, the only person approaching was this White guy dressed with a long leather coat buttoned at the waist only. The air was chilly and certainly an evening to be covered if not for aesthetics. His collar was turned up, with a chest full of hair exposed, emphasizing a long gold chain hung around his neck, dangling a large medallion. It was winter. I saw nothing else. I could barely keep my eyes off his hairy chest and attempted to concentrate on other exposed areas such as his face and hands. I heard nothing during what I think was a conversation we had. My eyes rolled from his chest to his dirty fingernails, the marks of which told a different story that conflicted with his "engineer" profession as stated in his online profile

Grateful for having my pager at hand, I indiscreetly turned it off and back on again to make it appear as if I were being paged to work. He responded immediately and appropriately with disappointment in my early departure, but continued eating as I walked out of the restaurant. I insisted on paying the bill since the fault was mine for ending the date early. I was glad to be out of the reaches of this "Shaq pretender". And he wasn't even Black and bald.

Needless to say, the matching agency could not find any suitable dates within the time frame of 6 months, so I was refunded my membership with a recommendation not to apply again.

GETTING IT RIGHT

I knew that God had other plans for me. I re-shifted my focus, and began to enjoy the friendships of the many visiting surgeons and colleagues working with me.

From Alberto the Italian, who was ever so kind and helpful, always there to assist, to Dr. Raoule and his wife, the loving Argentinians. As they learned the tricks of the trade, they were a welcomed addition to the transplant service. As with many visiting surgeons they initially became research fellows, later progressing to Clinical fellowship and Instructors in Surgery.

With the commitment to learn as much as possible and develop the skilled techniques of liver transplantation, many of these surgeons from South America (Brazil, Argentina, Venezuela), Europe (Spain, Italy, France) and Asia (Japan, China, Taiwan) remained at University of Pittsburgh for many months to years.

Dr. Starzl had the ability to obtain institutional privileges for them to operate, as nearly all were qualified practicing surgeons in their own institutions at home.

They became the scaffolding of the program, as many fellows can, and left after one or two years.

With the large accumulation of clinical cases, we had a wealth of information to gather for publications. Time was spent either operating or collecting data for presentation in abstracts. These opportunities were made available by the presence of many visiting surgeons with time on their hands.

No abstracts or papers could be sent for publication before meeting Dr. Starzl's approval. His 'red ink' edits were reliable predictors of the levels of revisions necessary for successful publication.

When my turn came, as with others, it required a trip to his office above the Pizza Hut. Written abstract - approved.

Required paper- completed. Presentation - practice session one - his office. Practice session two - transplant team members.

Arriving at the hotel for my presentation, Dr. Starzl again required another repeat of the same. By nightfall, it had created such insecurities that I stayed up all night practicing.

Still jittery by early AM, I was advised to take a half pill of Xanax. It was offered and I took it. By the time of my presentation at ten AM, I was unable to stand upright at the podium. I felt my body leaning over, fist under chin, giving my presentation in an extremely relaxed manner.

The endless rehearsal had proven worthwhile. I recalled little of what I uttered, and at the conclusion, watched as my body made its way back to my seat. Slumping in my chair, I refrained from making eye contact with any of my Pittsburgh colleagues.

Before the next session break, I was out of my chair, heading back to my room. I was going to crash, and I needed a soft surface to fall on. I awoke the next morning at 4 AM.

FINDING LOVE

As the only woman of color in the department of surgery, I was drawn to helping medical students for lectures and mentoring opportunities. It provided a sense of belonging to be able to connect with those who aspired to be doctors.

While working with the minority student office, Sherry, a young medical student, wanted to know if I would date older men.

"It would depend on how much older", I responded.

Within one week, she set up a conference call for me to talk to a visiting professor at University of Pittsburgh who was from Southern University, in her home state. She insisted we set up a date to meet. We did and, met a few days later for dinner.

We had dinner every day for the next four weeks. It was a match made in heaven.

Harvey was a true southern gentleman from North Carolina. He was on a one-year sabbatical leave from his job as Acting Dean at Southern University in Baton Rouge. After daily dates for over 2 months, we were sure life without each other would be impossible.

We were married six months after our 'blind date'. I surprised my parents, as they believed that I would not ever be interested in marriage and children.

My own rationalization was that life as a single career woman was not so bad, but life as a married woman with an incredible career was greater than I had ever imagined. My biological clock was also ticking as I was now thirty-two and wondering what a loss it would be to not have an offspring that could be just like me.

Harvey never returned to Southern University, but was hired by University of Pittsburgh, School of Public and International Affairs, to continue his work in International Development and Public Administration.

During the months of dating, I was approached with potential jobs offers. My years of training in Pittsburgh had left many of us with very low self-esteem. It was labeled the A.B.C. motto of transplant fellowship training: Affix Blame and Criticize.

With very little praise or appreciation for much of the work we did, I was left with the feeling of being less than capable of 'leaving the coop'. Offered a position at a southern program in Atlanta, I doubted my abilities to thrive in the South, and turned it down. Since moving to Brooklyn, the only other place I had lived outside of New York was Pittsburgh. I could not envision myself that far away from family. I knew nothing about the South.

Months later, Dr. Spencer came to Pittsburgh to learn about liver transplantation and to start his own liver program at his home institution. He remarked on how little appreciation I had for my remarkable skills and knowledge.

He opened my eyes to my own potential. I was a reason much of that potential did not rise to its greatest level. I would learn what it meant to be happy - being in that state of well-being with a clear purpose and tremendous satisfaction.

My duties in Pittsburgh were known and manageable. Staying worked well for our new marriage, career, and comfort.

NO OBLIGATION TO BACKWARD

By this time I was job seeking. Maybe I could move beyond Pittsburgh, and believe in myself as I had before.

A contact made years before, and the endorsement of that path by my mentor- tormentor, Dr. Starzl, gave me a new hope. It was possible that I could join a new transplantation program being started at another University Hospital.

Dr. Spencer had spent months in Pittsburgh getting the necessary mentorship to get this new program up and running.

There were patients selected for the first possible transplant. I learned about the possibilities of the program and was asked to help Dr. Spencer - a recent acquaintance and a friend of Dr. Starzl.

As part of the surgical team for the new program's first liver transplant, I was fortunate to have the more than able assistance and help of another senior attending, who also came from Pittsburgh.

For the University Hospital, it was an historic moment.

The first successful liver transplant was performed, opening up opportunities for many others.

I was offered a job as transplant surgeon at this hospital. I did not accept the job for several reasons. I failed my oral general surgery board examination. I had to repeat it, a few months later, to make things right.

There were other reasons.

I was an Assistant Professor at UPMC, and, the contract, offered by this hospital was for a much lower salary, and a position as a clinical instructor.

Here was the juggle. This was a nascent program, at a school looking to attain more prestige, offering a position with a lesser title in a city with a higher cost of living.

The University of Pittsburgh was where we had a house, where I had more to learn from Dr. Starzl, and was a long-established transplantation program. It offered me contact with transplant and pediatric transplant surgeons with ideas and opportunities around the world.

Even beyond the logic one can apply to deciding, I had a deep tingling feeling that a move from Pittsburgh, and the fledgling program at the University Hospital, was not God's plan for me.

There was one other female fellow who came to Pittsburgh to be qualified as a multi-organ transplant surgeon. Her name was Madison.

Dr. Starzl began to confuse us, as the two Black surgeons in transplant. We were the same height, body build, and, roughly, had the same deep, dark, chocolate complexion. Our hair styles were different; she had short-cropped, natural hair.

Madison was one of the first general surgery residents from that hospital who was interested in our Transplantation Fellowship Program.

On one particular day, Dr. Starzl called me to his office for a meeting. As he sat across from me, elbows perched on his knees with head tilted towards the floor, he was obviously disappointed in me. He believed I had an obligation to return to University Hospital. He said that Dr. Spencer had been instrumental in my training as a transplant surgeon.

He suggested that I owed a debt. A debt owed, as suggested, whether to a mentor, or to a race, is a burden.

This occurred after the potential job offer at the University Hospital, which would have been a demotion for me, and was declined after much consideration.

I attempted to correct Dr. Starzl, pointing out his mistake. The one who was trained by Dr. Spencer was Madison, not me. He had mixed us up again. I had to wonder if it was our similar appearance - or was there only one slot open to recognize a dark-skinned female surgeon at this level of achievement.

I mentored with, and did my surgery learning practice under Dr. Freeman, at Harlem hospital in New York City.

Dr. Starzl was still not hearing. He got up from his chair, still voicing his disappointment with me and still insisting I take the job. That was not an option for me, as it meant a cut in salary and a demotion from assistant professor, which I had just been granted.

I was not moving backward. No mentor should exact that as a fee.

I remained in Pittsburgh for the next twelve years.

I had the utmost respect for Dr. Starzl and was grateful for all that he had taught me as a surgeon. But I felt I still had a lot more to learn. The stars were not quite lined up for me to become a "big fish in small pond". Rather, I was a "small fish in a big pond" but wanted to continue to grow in a setting where the conditions were optimal. Dr. Starzl had an astonishing memory for details, and names. But, perhaps I was not being singled out. Maybe he really did think I was Madison. I kept hearing him refer to another Italian surgeon as "Rocky" for many months. His name was Alberto.

THE NEXT PHASE

Changes in the Department of General surgery resulted in a new Chairman of Surgery who had a strong background in transplantation. He saw a void that needed to be filled. The Pittsburgh Transplant Program lacked an emphasis on living kidney donation. He saw it as an essential component of kidney transplantation, of which Dr. Shapiro was in charge. I was selected to lead this program. We would alternate between performing both the living donor nephrectomy and the kidney implantation into the recipients.

For many years it was clear that Dr Starzl was opposed to living kidney donation. According to him, he had encountered some terrible complications with living kidney donors while he was in Denver, Colorado. With the increasing supply of deceased kidney donors, he explained, "No life should be placed in danger by donating a kidney while alive." He felt the risks were too great.

He explained that he had to testify for a potential living donor who had suffered an injury that resulted in loss of a leg. It was caused, solely, by a test required to qualify to be a living donor.

The living donor program brought an influx of pediatric transplants with organs donated primarily by parents. I gradually moved away from the liver transplant service, focusing on my new responsibility. Dr. Starzl eventually embraced the use of living donors and even referred one of his long-term successful liver transplant recipients. That patient would undergo one of the first combined bone marrow-kidney transplants, with the organ and marrow being donated by the patient's brother. It would be the start of a new era.

MOTHERHOOD

I was about to have our first child. Was I going to be a great mother? How would I know if I had the skills to do this? I was the last of seven children, with little experience taking care of babies. I had done many jobs as a babysitter, but they all were toddlers. What I knew was how to operate as a surgeon.

My first trimester was plagued with constant nausea, and all-day sickness. I ate to dampen the nausea, equipped with an endless supply of crackers and cold milk. As the baby grew, the response of my (then) one hundred twenty-five pound frame could feel each inner muscle as my tissues accommodated my enlarging uterus.

Pregnancy was truly draining. It sapped my energy and by the early afternoon I had to rest. The 'Joys of Pregnancy' failed to disclose that this new life growing inside would not only cause nausea, heartburn and bloating, but dizziness that occurred when operating. The constant motion of shifting positions made each case more difficult.

Pregnancy and the smell of old blood was not a good combination. It was made worse once the blood dried on the cotton drapes; and got to the repulsive stage for me. The long hours of liver transplantation were most difficult. I ached all over but most particularly my back. I gradually shifted away from livers to the shorter cases of kidney transplantation. The atmosphere at this time created an opportunity for me to spend more on a less time-consuming service such as kidney and pancreas transplant.

As time grew closer to the delivery date, the more apprehensive and frightened I became. Being a physician, I had too much knowledge that contributed to my fear of one hundred and one things going wrong. What if she was unhealthy? Or deformed?

We knew it was a girl - I needed to know the sex. I wanted to be prepared. The idea of readying a room with green or yellow to be neutral and not knowing the sex was unreasonable. I needed to be prepared and ready.

There certainly was a price to pay as a result of being on call and trying to maintain a semblance of normalcy. My brain was suffering – 'pregnancy brain' syndrome with forgetfulness and delayed thought processes that made me miserable with concern.

Would I ever recover from this?

I questioned my physician. "Don't worry. It will improve after delivery."

As I entered my last trimester, I had to start making plans for my time off.

The question to my chairman was how much time I was allowed off for maternity leave. There was nothing in the department bylaws as there was no precedent for this until now. Beside me, there was only one additional female surgeon in the department.

We agreed it would be the same as it was for the nurses: 6 weeks. With a rough delivery, an episiotomy, and a broken coccyx, I was wishing for much more.

When I informed Dr. Starzl that I would be off for 6 weeks, he remarked with astonishment.

"Why so long? Betsy (the other Caucasian female transplant surgeon at the time) just had a baby and she was right back to work in a week!"

I replied: "Sorry sir. But, I'm not Betsy. I'll be out for 6 weeks."

MARRIAGE AND CHILDREN

Our first born, Akela, arrived the Friday before Memorial Day weekend. Life was not easy that first week, or month, or year.

We were home by Sunday, without a breast pump or instructions on how to use it. My milk chose to come in before our new infant was interested. Engorged and in pain, I sent my husband to find any drugstore that was still open at 7 PM on the first weekend of the summer.

He batted zero. My last resort was my colleague Bob. They had their first child 6 months earlier. In fact, his wife had passed on all her maternity dresses. With her help, I was rescued from a potential breast explosion.

In those days, I was given little to no instruction on breastfeeding, except, put the baby on the breast and let her latch on. However, she was not doing what was expected. I was mostly in pain. Where were the instructions to get this infant to take the breast milk? I gave it a good try and resorted to supplementing my milk with baby formula. Akela finally stopped crying. The child was starving and I was failing terribly at being a model mother. I had imagined breastfeeding full-time for months. I knew of the benefits of mother's milk and was determined I would be proud of myself as a working, breastfeeding mother. With the little milk I was able to produce, I reserved breast feedings for nighttime. With bleeding, chapped nipples, I was unable to endure and breastfeed our daughter beyond a month. I had failed this part of motherhood.

I returned to the pediatric surgery service after my maternity leave. My daughter survived on baby formula, and I pumped what little breast milk I was producing during the day. It was incredibly hard to eat and drink the amount needed to maintain my milk supply. The battle was between trying to drop the baby fat and producing milk for my child. Never a big eater, it was a struggle, because my mind told me, 'you need to lose the weight'. I ate salads for lunch the entire year post-delivery.

As I made my daily rounds, the cry of each infant would immediately create a maternal response to lactate, and I would immediately have to take action. I invested in tons of breast pads as I tried to save all those fabulous silk shirts from pre-motherhood. So much for being stylish.

Motherhood also brought with it postpartum depression and guilt. The strength and tenacity that propelled me to my current level was not a match for the mental havoc brought on by my hormonal disturbance. Should I have taken more time before coming back to work? What if I cannot be home tonight? Who can I call on for help?

Thank God for friendship. I am forever in debt to Dr. Diane. She listened to my concerns, offered sympathy and understanding and was never judgmental. She offered her shoulder for me to cry on, which seemed like every day for the first month I was back on duty.

While her main focus was pediatric surgery, she became my colleague, friend and was my trusted assistant on the majority of cases I did, both in adults and children. She accompanied me on donor retrieval cases, and was there with us when the first and second liver transplants were performed at an outside hospital.

It was during a pediatric liver transplant case that it occurred. She contracted Hepatitis C. Referred to at that time as non-A, non-B Hepatitis.

A young patient, while on the operating table, was having difficulty maintaining his blood pressure while his new liver was being implanted. Blood was requested, and given to increase the blood pressure. It was not running as fast as desired. To increase the rate of flow, the anesthesiologist was instructed by the surgeon to pump the blood in as fast as possible. With that, he increased the pressure on the bag of blood. Positioned near the drapes that separated us from the anesthesiologists, the bag of blood ruptured. She was squirted as the blood splashed over her neck and shoulder region.

Despite wearing glasses, a small drop was all that was necessary to curve around the angle of her frames to enter her eye.

Diane was later diagnosed with, and treated for, that Hepatitis C. Fortunately, she has continued to do well, with no long-lasting sequela.

Managing life as a transplant surgeon and mother was not easy. With no family close, it meant finding a sitter quickly. Diane was always willing to help, when she was available. While she had no children of her own, her motherly instincts were quite sharp.

Being new to Pittsburgh I struggled to find 'good help'. Students were often available but were not dependable for most emergencies. My husband was a Kellogg Fellow at the time, and spent much of his time traveling.

It was suggested by a trauma doctor that I hire two nannies: each one would work 12 hours, taking care of the baby and "I would have it made". That's how he and wife raised their children.

But who would be raising our daughter? That was out of the question. Perhaps one full-time nanny might be an option. Harvey was not agreeable to having another person living in our home.

So, we resorted to a daytime nanny.

Having one child seemed much more manageable than having two. Grocery shopping or dining out was not so bad. I could just place Akela in the shopping cart and off we would go. Dining with one child to keep quiet was reasonable. It was much more difficult with two children.

I was thirty-four years old when I had Akela. Knowing we would have another child, the fear of the possibility of having a genetic abnormality with a pregnancy over age thirty-five was real. I could not shake it.

Waiting was not an option. We weighed the risks, which seemed small. Our doctors reassured us that there was little to worry about. But we still opted for amniocentesis and felt reassured.

By my second pregnancy I had learned the art of operating with a big belly. In the first six months it was easier to work with the operating table down and my stomach leaning on the table. Operating room tables are very narrow, fitting the average person with their hands down at their sides, tucked partially under. If the patient was large, or there was no room to lean on the table, then it meant operating with my side against the table, which was most uncomfortable.

In my eighth to ninth month, the best position was with the table higher. However, it meant shifting positions during the necessary bladder relief breaks.

As the baby grew along with my abdomen, I would warn my obese patients that they were in competition with my stomach, and I would be charging them extra for the suffering my unborn child had to endure by being compressed during surgery.

In several living donor transplants with the chairman of surgery, he would often be frustrated by my constant need to take bathroom breaks. He even suggested that I have a Foley catheter placed before each case to prevent my constant request for relief. He was joking, I thought. I gave it strong consideration by declined the offer.

By the end of my ninth month in the second pregnancy, I was experiencing significant hip pain that would cause me to buckle and potentially fall. I opted to stay at home the last week.

I was ready to have this baby enter its new world.

SHOPPING WHILE BLACK

It was nearly the last week of my second pregnancy and, along with my student matchmaker who came over to visit, we took a neighborhood walk. Our path was just a couple of short blocks from my home to the local shopping area. It was a leisurely stroll of just roaming about and window-shopping.

As befit the time and circumstance, we entered the Baby's-R-Us to simply browse. Upon exiting we wandered into another store, still just looking. While searching the racks in the back of the store, a policewoman tapped me on my shoulder and asked if we could step out of the store. Asked why, she stated the need to talk to us outside.

"Two women recently robbed the Baby's R US store down the street, and you and your friend match the description given by the store manager", she said.

"Who us? What are we being accused of?" I declared this with no lack of surprise, or indignation, in my voice.

"Taking items from the store without paying.", the policewoman said matter-of-factly.

"Shoplifting? Are you kidding me? Where did you think I am hiding these items?", under my shirt? This is a genuine pregnancy", I said. And, with that, I lifted my top to show the policewoman.

The policewoman was unimpressed, and said, "I'm sorry Miss. But, you will need to accompany me back to the store. You can ride in the police car if you want."

With that she attempted to walk me over to the police wagon. Since it was a one- way street, it meant driving around the block. There was no way I was getting in the wagon.

I voiced that I would walk, and she accompanied me and the student back to the store. Crowds had now gathered, as we were seen as robbers; no evidence, no trial, only the word of someone we had never seen.

Though more than highly embarrassed, I kept my composure, but knew my heart rate was rapid and my adrenalin was at a high point. There were few persons of color walking or shopping this day in this particular neighborhood. Quaint, small and upscale, I search the faces of those who dared to look our way. With a quick glance, they turned away, avoiding obvious judgement of guilty or not.

Arriving back at the Baby's-R-Us store, we stood outside as the manager was called to see if we were indeed the shoplifters.

The Caucasian manager came out, took a look at us, and stated: "No, that's not them.". He turned and walked back into the store.

The nonchalant attitude of the policewoman continued. "Sorry Miss. You're free to go.", she said.

With only a half-hearted 'sorry' to carry, we walked through the crowds and returned to my home, angry and embarrassed. With only my house keys, I could not have proved who I was. I was never asked either. It did not matter. We were Black women, shopping in an elite neighborhood.

The likely common assumption: Black, women, thieves. No one assumed Black, woman, surgeon.

DIFFERENT PERFECTIONS - CHALLENGES AT HOME

The time frame from knowing there is a kidney donor, to the actual arrival of the organ, could be as much as twelve to fifteen hours.

That was enough time to find a sitter who did not have to work the next day or had to be at school by a certain hour.

Life as a kidney transplant surgeon gave me more flexibility than doing liver transplantations. It was still my intention to return to liver transplantation, once the kids were older. At least that is what I told myself. However, I knew having a family came with personal sacrifices. My sacrifice would be remaining available for our girls.

But having two children was enough for me. With long working hours, it was difficult staying awake when at home. I felt guilty about having to use the television as a 'sitter' so I could take a quick nap.

Despite the initial objections of my spouse to having a 'live-in' nanny, we had to give it consideration. No one in our families, no one in our 'village' was closer than six hours away from Pittsburgh.

Finally, we found Ms. Brenda. She was sent from God to save us. I could take a deep breath, even take a trip to window shop (with caution).

Being on the kidney service had advantages. With the busy operating room schedule, and the ability of kidneys to be preserved for longer times, kidney transplants were not given as high a priority as transplants of livers.

I would often be told my case would have to be delayed. I would return home in the evenings, to be with my family. After putting the children to bed, I would venture to the hospital for an 11 PM start time. With the change of shift at midnight, I would be lucky to get started at one in the morning.

The primary requirement I had was to have my case completed by five in the morning, so I could return home before our girls awoke. It was part of my ritual. Unaware that I was even absent, they would be up and off to school without missing a beat. This would become a standard night shift routine for me.

However, I rescheduled the timing of evening operations so I could be present for most of the after-school events. Harvey did what he could when he was at home and not traveling.

Our girls might have missed out on Girl Scouts, but they were both part of Brownie troops. Aisha wanted dance classes and did well with music lessons; Akela wanted to be a gymnast. As they grew, we tried to accommodate their extracurriculars.

Annual conferences, for all types of networking, continuing education, and idea exchange in the medical community, are necessary and expected parts of life in this career. Transplantation-focused careers, and the conferences one needs to attend to stay abreast and get ahead, require even more careful selections for conferencing.

Attending these carefully chosen events meant taking one of the two girls. Whether it was to the Miami winter meeting or one in Arizona, it was coupled with some special time alone with that child. Each girl relished the rare one-on-one time together. Family vacations were built around conferences, allowing some extra days for non-academic activities.

We had both girls attend the Stanton Lab School, located close to work for both of us.

It was academically challenging. It was prestigious. It was the best choice to give them the foundation to achieve, or even over-achieve, in academics. This was familiar territory for me, and for Harvey.

In the family we built, as in the families that built us, education was key, mandatory, and our greatest weapon.

SHOCK

The Lab School contacted us with shocking information. Our elder girl failed the second grade! How does a 7 year-old fail second grade?

The teacher told us, "Akela does not pay attention in class. She sits in the back and talks all the time!"

"When did this all start? Nothing was ever said to us!", was all we felt we could say.

"We noticed that Akela was having difficulty with some of the students in her class. And, she does not do any work in class. Her papers have scribbles across each line instead of words.", the teacher relayed.

With some consternation, we replied, "So, why do these papers, all with scribbles across them, have green check marks at the top, and 'Great Job' written on them?"

The teacher responded, only, with, "Perhaps the student aide was not paying attention when she graded the papers."

From us, came the following, "So, are you telling us that her inability to complete her in-class work has been missed for months? If she has some form of learning disability, should she not be tested?"

"We don't feel she needs to be tested. But, you can have it done if you wish to know. It's our conclusion that she should repeat second grade.", the teacher stately flatly.

A more forceful reply, from us, was needed, and came: "We will certainly have her tested, because we need answers, even if you don't!"

The next week Akela came home with some of her test papers, still with scribbles instead of words.

We read each one, as best as we could.

On the side of one of her papers, other second graders, we believe, who could spell very well, had written:

"You are a BLACK BITCH."

We demanded a meeting with the parents of the child who wrote it. The teacher refused, stating they would speak to the parent, but did not want us to confront the parents. The parent was a teacher at the same school. We were overreacting. Perhaps being a little sensitive? It was clearly not their child, and clearly with reversed roles, our daughter would have been reprimanded or even expelled.

Our children were taken out of the school. Akela was diagnosed with Attention Deficit Disorder (ADD). She also had an additional component of hyperactivity.

As a mother you begin to think that, perhaps, it was something you did or did not do to cause her learning disability. Yes, my pregnancy with Akela was stressful emotionally and physically. There were long working hours. There were late nights and sleepless nights. And yes, I carried the guilt.

We started with behavior modification because it was taboo to put such a young child on medication. She worked consistently with a therapist.

Over and over, we were told: 'She will, eventually, grow out of it.'

Less than one year later, Akela had a grand mal seizure while she was asleep. She had no fever, no infections; there was no discernible cause. A second one occurred in the emergency room that night. A scan of the head showed no abnormalities.

For the next 2 years, near the end of Spring, April to May, she would have another seizure. Each time, the cause was unknown.

Her diagnosis was modified to Attention Deficit Hyperactivity Disorder (ADHD), as the hyperactivity was noticeable but still overshadowed by her attention deficit. Four years later, there were no signs of the symptoms diminishing.

We chose to pursue multiple options, simultaneously. We worked with professionals and kept Akela in intense behavior modification therapy while becoming resentful about coverage for possible seizures. We followed the recommended dietary restrictions. She attended special schools for a more focused program tailored to her particular needs.

No thought was given to any medication for ADHD, due to possible contraindication with seizure medications.

Harvey was still a traveling scholar, while working full time at the University. I was still a transplant surgeon. We still had another daughter - Aisha.

Akela's situation weighed heavily on me, as constant school meetings were required. Neurologists were needed to monitor her seizure medications. And, there were the weekly meetings with the therapist.

Aisha, the younger child, was feeling neglected, and becoming resentful. She was at times downright hateful toward her sister, likely for demanding so much of our attention.

"Why does she have to come with us wherever we go?" "Can't she stay at home with Ms. Brenda?"

When questioned why she did not want Akela around when we go out together, she responded, "She had time alone with you for 2 years before I came along. So, I should have 2 years worth of time with you, and without her, to make it even." Aisha was only 6 years old at the time.

The guilt is always there. Perhaps I could have done better. Did the stress of work emotionally contribute to the learning disability and later diagnosis of bipolar disorder in my firstborn? Was it something I failed to eat? Was it lack of appropriate rest during my pregnancy?

I will never, really, know.

The question always asked of me is: "Are your children following in your footsteps?"

That answer is simple. No way.

They think I continue to work too hard. They are both artistic, with no interest in the field of medicine. They will be supported in whatever they choose to take on. Within reason, that is.

ADMITTING DEPRESSION

My first struggle with depression was in my fellowship. There was work, work, and work.

Paul, my friend and a coordinator in the surgery fellowship program, called us 'A,B,C'. He saw what we did, in 'the Pittsburgh Transplant Program', as – Affix, Blame, and Criticize.

There was little praise given for the good things you did, but always a question, "Who messed up this time?"

I was losing the little self-esteem I accumulated before arriving, and by the second year of fellowship, I had very little.

It came to a point where I had to turn to my faith to keep me going. At times, it seemed even that was not be enough. The negative forces worked their way into my brain. I had cut a phrase from a magazine and taped it to my dresser mirror. It read: 'YES I CAN'. It was 1988, long before Obama ran his campaign on a similar theme.

I barely achieved the level of confidence and enthusiasm that the very positive message was designed to deliver. Happiness and bliss were short-lived, even in the few times they presented themselves to me. The dark head of depression was raised too often in those years, and then in the years beyond. I blamed it on the start of menopause, even though I wasn't even close to age forty.

Overall, I started to doubt my own skills and capabilities during most of my fellowship years. To me, it felt like all of this had to be faced alone; there was no one with whom I could speak. I also did not want to appear weak and 'not having what it takes' to be a surgeon. One day, as I was scrubbed in for a kidney transplant, with one of the young urologists. He was very open about his use of Prozac. He talked about his own struggles in life, his family, and work.

With his South American accent, and humor, he stated, "I know my Prozac is working when I stop worrying about everything. Then, I am at the point when 'I don't give a damn!'" That sealed it for me.

Instead of submitting to constant emotional outbursts, low self-esteem, and not confronting my demons, I began trials of Johnson's Wort which was said to help with depression and mood disorders. I waited quite a while to see a response from this medication, but saw little response. In fact, my memory became worse. I could only describe the sense of being 'stupider' and depressed, which was worse than being depressed alone. It had to go down the drain.

Eventually, as the years went by, I swallowed my pride and approached my own doctor about my low morale, constant anger and feelings of despair. I was started on Celexa which made a remarkable difference in my outlook on life. However, I felt ashamed that I was taking an antidepressant, and would often use the excuse that it was really for my hot flashes. That made it more acceptable. Without the formal diagnosis of depression, I felt I did not have to include it on various forms that are required for health information.

Admitting to having depression seemed degrading. I know that many people had beliefs about depression that were reduced to phrases, such as: 'He/she has nothing to be depressed about. They have everything - a great job, big house and everything someone else would appreciate.'

To them, even to me at the time, the world saw a surgeon. Therefore, I had nothing to be depressed about!

I should have been able to pat myself on the back with congratulations. I should have been able to dismiss the way colleagues shifted my name down the line of authors on papers where my contributions were greater. I should have been able to handle constant rejection by patients who requested another physician because of color of my skin.

Too often I heard, "Don't let that get to you." No one who said those things was in my shoes.

Intermittently, I would feel well and make the assumption that I could get off the Celexa. Happiness would continue for about 2 weeks before the wall would rise again.

Starting over took another 2-3 weeks to reach effective levels before I could feel better again.

Motherhood exacerbated the depression. Crying babies, a traveling husband, being away from family with few friendships outside of work – none of these were boosts.

One Saturday, an unknown car pulled into our driveway. An African-American woman got out and introduced herself. I stood and introduced myself; I was working in the garden. She was a God-send. She knew I was new in town, without family, and she came to help me with the children. She explained that she would be around to give me a break, sometimes on weekends, whenever I needed it.

Yes, I needed it. I thanked God for sending her my way. She was there every Saturday morning; whenever she was available, she was there to help.

I continued to occasionally convince myself that I did not need to medicate. However, I failed miserably and had to restart every time. I had to admit that I was not at fault. I was not causing myself to be depressed. I had what friends would called 'everything' and there was no reason for me to be depressed.

Yet, I was.

Now, I take my Celexa every night. When I see a patient who is facing depression and does not want to take medication, I explain that it's their body that is not producing the right hormones. It is not a fault of the mind. Depression is a physical, medical condition.

I tell them my story, and that of my Spanish colleague. I tell them that I take antidepressants, and I too, have to live with the stigma of having such a disorder.

But, without medication, I have the face some of the dwarfs that sit on the desk of my gynecologist: Bitchy, Grumpy, Moody, Forgetful, and Psycho. I don't like any of those monikers. Not taking the medication is not worth it.

Now, I don't sweat the small stuff. My husband complains about my shoes left in various rooms, about my clothes still at the foot of bed. My response is some form of: "If it bothers you, take them up." "Or I'll get around to it".

This wall of physical betrayal, by my own body, would not stand either. I refuse to give on scaling a wall I know I have the tools to conquer.

Exercise helps. And yes, I have a lot of shoes. And clothes too!

RISING IN PITTSBURGH

It soon became known that the first Black, female transplant surgeon in this country was living right in the City of Pittsburgh.

I was immediately embraced by multiple civic and social organizations throughout the region. I had not given much thought to being the first in the field. I was there for a purpose, to fulfill my passion to be a surgeon. This was my drive and I valued my ability to be able to get to this point in my career. But I still had a long way to go.

From the Pittsburgh Courier to the Post-Gazette, I was recognized for my achievements and celebrated.

Pregnant with our second child, I was selected for the 1992 Celebration of Excellence by the Triangle Corner Limited honors, as one of four women chosen for their achievements. Both my chairman and Ernestine Marsh nominated me for this award. I was deeply honored.

In my eighth month of pregnancy, I recalled walking onto the stage and with great surprise, my heart skipped a beat. There sat a large, low very comfortable couch for us to sit on. There was no way I could sit on that couch and gracefully get to my feet without a great deal of embarrassment. As if sensing my hesitation to sit, I was brought a regular high back chair.

Someone was reading my thoughts!

The Pittsburgh Chapter of the Links, Incorporated immediately welcomed me into their sisterhood of professional women. Nationally, the Links Incorporated is one of the oldest and largest volunteer service organizations committed to strengthening our communities through service. I welcomed the connection to a new circle of women of color, and the ability to gain valuable knowledge and guidance while living in Pittsburgh.

In 1996, I was awarded the Carlow College Women of Spirit Award for my work with students at that time. I was among notable women, such as Lois Wholey, Marcia Martin and Susan Bohn, just to name a few.

The National Kidney Foundation of Western Pennsylvania awarded me the 'Gift of Life Award' in 1998. It was presented by Dr. Thomas Starzl himself. I also had the honor of having my father attend this event. He was extremely proud of my accomplishments.

I was inducted into a Hall of Fame - twice: The United Negro College Fund - Achievers Hall of Fame award, and The National Minority Transplant Hall of Fame - Transplant Pioneer Award.

In addition, I received two Honorary Degrees. I received a Doctor of Science from Seton Hill College of Pennsylvania (1997), and one from Long Island University (Brooklyn Campus) in 1998.

While talking with the students at Long Island University, one student wanted to know my age. After stating I was 42 years of age, she remarked, "Gosh, I was just being born the year you graduated!"

"Yes indeed. I could be your mother." I replied.

While that was indeed physically possible, I would be given the honor of being a daughter: A 'Distinguished Daughter of Pennsylvania'. I was honored by Governor Tom Ridge and his wife Michelle Ridge.

Since 1949, outstanding women have been honored for their extraordinary service and contributions to the Commonwealth of Pennsylvania. I was chosen as one of those women.

I was most grateful for having both my parents attend the award ceremony at the Governor's residence in Harrisburg. My dad's excitement to be in the presence of the other awardees, who were notable judges, philanthropists, educators, and many others was obvious. He exhibited endless smiles of happiness for all that I had accomplished. My parents were, both, truly excited to be pictured with the Governor of Pennsylvania. The girls, ages four and six, were hopelessly bored.

"WHY DO YOU NEED MORE MONEY?" MY FIGHT FOR PROMOTION AND EQUAL PAY

This was the question asked of me during a meeting regarding my promotion. I had been an Assistant Professor of Surgery in the Department of Surgery for years. My male colleagues in transplantation had all been granted positions as Associate Professors in Surgery.

Each of us took advantage of the equal opportunities for publications, and to present at National conferences. Unless one had previous grant funding to support continued bench research as a transplant surgeon, your contract was renewed annually. There was no long-term commitment. Proving one's worth was necessary.

Equal opportunity, and equity, were not recognized as different. Even the order selection for listing authors in publications made this obvious.

On multiple occasions I would bring attention to my name being shifted down the line of authors. It seemed a natural pattern for a male colleague to add his male co-workers ahead of my name. They had each other. Who would be my advocate?

If one, brings attention to blatant biased behavior, you are labeled as 'being too sensitive'.

Yes, I was sensitive about my career and my advancement.

In one instance, I had collected data, written the abstract and it was accepted for publication. I was rewarded with the ability to present, but I could not be primary author. This was my data. This was unequal bias. This was the early 1990's.

I had compiled a list of answers to the anticipated questions before I met to discuss my deserved promotion. At the same time there was voiced displeasure from another Caucasian female general surgeon about not being promoted to Associate Professor level.

It was not about whether I 'needed' more money or not. It was about my right to be promoted based on my credentials and my fulfillment of the required expectations. The same criteria for promotion applied to both men and women in the department. So why did my male colleagues have no issues in moving up the ladder of success?

As women in medicine or surgery, we fail at appropriately negotiating salaries when hired. When hired as a Clinical Instructor, and even as an Assistant Professor, there was no salary negotiation and discussion. I was ignorant and not schooled in such financial matters. It was not taught as part of career management in medical school. I had never given it any degree of deep analysis. I was naïve enough to believe that such issues did not exist. I believed, falsely, that I had reached a level where there was a true meritocracy.

Happy to be making more of a salary than that of a fellow, I was more focused on mastering my craft than paying attention to how much I was being compensated for my work.

Sitting across from my chairman, I stood my ground. My deserved promotion was not just about money. It was not about whether my husband made a good living and between the two of us we should be 'well off'. None of those things mattered.

I did not want to think that the system was unfair, but it surely appeared to be. Why was it easier and quicker for the male surgeons to navigate their way up the ladder?

Having not negotiated my last salary, I was aware that my annual salary was certainly not close to being equal to the male surgeons.

But just how would I provide proof of unequal pay for men and women? Those on the other side of the negotiating table were not willing to disclose what they paid my peers; and, neither were those white male peers. So, without specific data for verification, there was just speculation.

About the same time, the University had been placed in the spotlight for having appallingly small numbers of women at the Professorship level. It was a system wide problem that was only beginning to be addressed. There was only one woman of color who had moved through the ranks to the level of full professor at the Medical School.

I won the battle for my promotion to Associate Professor of Surgery. Having started off with a below average salary, mostly from my own ignorance and failure to see the system as inequitable, I cannot stress how important it is to research your position and the average salary paid before accepting your offer. I did not.

As if to compensate for the inability of the system to compensate me on an equal level as the male surgeons, I was gifted a lovely antique ladies brooch, once owned by the mother of my leader and mentor for this stage of my career. Maybe it was a gesture of appreciation for my talents. I would like to believe so.

There are politics in the transplantation community, and its sub-communities. Contacts, learnings, and obligation get complicated.

I revered, and still revere Dr. Starzl's skills and dedication. Whether he confused me with Madison or not, how would women of color move beyond being silhouettes in the room?

In many ways, without a new approach to mentorship, women, men, anyone in medicine, may remain silhouettes in the room for some time to come.

Yet, given funding, time and determination, some things work. During my tenure at the University of Pittsburgh we trained many more Black male fellows in our program.

The program at the University Hospital did survive and continued their liver transplant program despite the choice I made.

Many years later, another female resident would come to Pittsburgh to do research in pediatric surgery. She would embrace transplantation as a career. She moved on to complete her transplant fellowship at University of California, Los Angeles.

She would become the third African-American female transplant surgeon in this country.

REACHING ACROSS THE SEAS

BARBADOS

The first kidney transplant was performed at Queen Elizabeth Hospital in Barbados, my homeland, on June 14th, 1987. Ten years later, the program had performed only 10 living donor kidney transplants.

I was in a position to offer my services to my country and, with much enthusiasm, I reached out to those in charge of the program. In 1998 I was invited to Barbados for a series of lectures and updates in organ transplantation.

My presence was well received. It resulted in several return visits over the next ten years. I was proud to be able to increase awareness about the rising incidence of kidney disease on the island.

From community lectures to newspaper articles, I offered education relating to the increasing number of patients with kidney failure on the island. Two successful living donor kidney transplants were performed at Christiana Care in Delaware. The patients have returned to Barbados, and continue to do well. While living donation of kidneys is acceptable, the concept of using organs from brain dead individuals is still hotly debated.

The kidney transplant program, intermittently, performed a few living donor transplants over the next ten years, with their own surgeons as well as visiting surgeons from England.

Years later, I would be selected by the Order of Barbados (National Honours System of the Government of Barbados) to receive the Gold Crown of Merit (GCM) honor.

The highest honor bestowed is to be a Knight, or Dame, of St. Andrew (Sir or Dame), followed by the Companion of Honour of Barbados (The Honourable).

My hard work and dedication, and I assume 'giving back' to my country of origin and communities paid off. I can now use the post-nominal letters, GCM. The medal was bestowed by the Governor-General of Barbados.

SUDAN

Mohammed was an aspiring surgeon. He, graduated in his country and came to the University of Pittsburgh to learn about transplantation. He had not completed a surgery residency, and therefore had much difficulty as a transplant fellow.

The expectation was that he would return to Khartoum to perform kidney transplants. Patients in both places were registered, and being worked up to undergo living donation and transplantation. Donors and recipients were already being matched in anticipation of his return.

Because of the 'walls' of paperwork associated with authorizing Mohammed to perform the needed surgeries in his skill set, a group from Pittsburgh would go to perform the surgeries.

A four-surgeon team, led by Dr. Fung, was accompanied by nurses charged with post-operative patient care. I was one of those surgeons.

We met the Sudanese team of doctors at the Hilton hotel, including the anesthesiologists. The days were humid, bright and uncontrollably sweaty. The sun was inescapably hot.

Our schedule dictated that we would be sheltered from the relentless heat that runs in waves over every part of the Sudan desert and its brown adobe cities.

We planned to perform two living donor transplants a day, for the five business days we were scheduled to be there.

Despite the temperatures, soaring over 105 degrees Fahrenheit, even at night, I was told to respect the customs for women, to cover arms and legs, wear skirts, no pants. The days under the blue lights would be long.

The heat rose from the hard dirt, stone, and sand colored concrete of the city streets. With respect for our host, we would endure the long nights as well.

The first gathering occurred in the hotel on the first night. As we waited for one of the last nurses to arrive, all heads turned to see her coming towards in ... in ... shorts! Not Bermuda shorts, short-shorts!

Our host was about to have a heart attack, as the other residents looked over in shock. I was asked quietly to have her change her outfit to prevent an intervention for others. I did.

The assumption was that the surgery would start at 8 AM; the finish was projected to be 1 PM. We would start again at 3 PM, and finish by 7 PM.

The reality was quite different. The anesthesiology team arrived at 8:45 AM. Alcohol prep pads were prohibited. This was understood, as was the admonishment for the women on our team to wear long dresses, no pants, no shorts - and to cover our arms.

The ban on all things with alcohol would have quite different outcomes, though. There was a secret stash of those cleansing, disinfecting pads, brought in by one of residents. At least a few patients would get the benefits, until the stash ran out.

There was no automatic anesthesia machine. The team had to hand-ventilate the patient throughout the case.

The scrub nurses spoke no English. So, asking for specific instruments, any instruments, was a forced exercise in pointing, drawing shapes in the air, or trying to learn - on-the-fly - the Arabic names for some of the tools.

Most patients were Christians. At least one Muslim patient refused to have me operate on him unless I converted to the Islam religion.

One of my colleagues interpreted.

"He wants to know if you will do your best to have a successful operation?"

My comment was, "Absolutely! I will do my utmost best!"

I was nodding my head to add a visual buttress to my emphatic yes response. The interpreter let me know that the patient agreed to allow us to proceed with the operation.

"He said that's great. He will put his trust in you."

The transplant went well and as we sat down that night to have dinner, the interpreter shocked us.

He said, "I have a confession to make. Unfortunately, the patient this morning would not let you perform the operation unless you convert to Islam. I told him you would and you gave me the response he wanted to see and hear.

"By saying yes, you agreed to change your religion. Otherwise there was no way he would let you operate.

"I apologize, but we needed to get the surgery done. I'm so sorry Dr. Scantlebury!"

With that, he came over to give me a hug, seeing that my face could not hide my discontent.

There was something lighter though. My husband declared, "Now that you have hugged her, you know you have to marry her, by Islamic law!"

It was a needed joke.

While we were able to complete two cases in one day, we realized we did not have the personnel to have eight patients be cared for after the operations; it could not be done - well - by one nurse.

We also did not have the technology to turn over the operating room quickly enough to get the second case started before 4 PM.

Linens used in the operating room had to be hand washed. There was no sterilization machine. We resorted to paper drapes for the next 4 cases.

Flies invaded our operating rooms. Fortunately, no patients developed infections.

Instruments were hand washed. They were boiled in a big stainless-steel pot. It was the closest we could get to proper sterilization.

Since alcohol was prohibited in the country, and because we had exhausted the secret stash of alcohol wipes, we resorted to another 'trick'. We used 4x4 gauze, cut into 2x2 inch squares; then we would soak them in some purchased, 'bootleg' alcohol.

At least once, there was an electricity outage during a surgical case. I was implanting the kidney; my husband was playing the role of recording photographer. Things went dark and Harvey instantly became 'spotlight holder'. He, literally, had my back; standing behind me with needed lighting (and support) throughout the remainder of the case.

With all the challenges we faced, we were only able to complete six living donor kidney transplants instead of ten. The remaining families, who camped out in front of the hospital, were disappointed. We were disappointed also.

The nursing staff volunteered to stay behind to make sure the remaining patients in the hospital were monitored appropriately. We returned home after visiting with government officials and taking in a few sightseeing adventures.

The Sudan experience was a challenge, an adventure, a 'wall', an education, and one of the most gratifying experiences of my career.

YEARS OF TRAVEL - CHERISHED

From my first opportunity to travel as a medical student, I embraced being away from home as a method for de-stressing. With each place visited came new experiences, deeper cultural awareness, and a lot less anxiety.

There was no time to travel outside of donor runs, and mandated conferences that could cut any time for relaxation short by a call for your presentation. Fortunately, Harvey also had a love of travel.

We found ways to use the cherished time.

Our first trip together was to the Philippines.

I had a patient named Sachin, who was taken home to the islands by her parents. They wanted her intravenous catheter removed. They trusted no one locally to perform the procedure. They requested a surgeon from Children's Hospital, in Pittsburgh.

The surgeon originally requested was unable to travel at the time needed. I was volunteered, and accepted gladly.

We were flown, first-class, to Manila, housed in a Four Star hotel, and, were given the grand treatment. The catheter was removed successfully, and we were given a three-day trip in Hong Kong before our return home. It was a lifestyle I could get used to, but could not afford.

As the recipient of a Kellogg Leadership, Harvey traveled to Africa at least once a year, sometimes twice or even three times. While working for the USAID project, to help historically disadvantaged institutions in South Africa, I was able to accompany him in 1994. This was before Apartheid was dismantled.

South Africa was only one of a few countries in Sub-Saharan Africa where transplantation, kidney transplantation, programs and practices were well established and underway.

The first two kidney transplants were performed in 1986, fourteen years after the first successful transplant in the United States. The team was led by Dr. Starzl and South African surgeon Dr. Bert Myburgh. The surgeries were successful, but both patients died due to rejection.

Fortunately, having trained with one of the country's surgeons at UPMC, I was able to visit South African facilities, and learn more about their system. Administering anti-rejection medications was a luxury for their patients. After the first year those drugs were provided only on a limited basis, then the medications were tapered off. There was little to no additional assistance for those patients. The first year was most critical.

From Ghana to Ethiopia, I accompanied Harvey as he took on the role of 'Chairperson of the Consortium for International Policy and Development (CIMPAD). As well, Harvey was made President of the American Society for Public Administration. I accompanied on a trip to China. While at the Great Wall many of the Chinese tourists wanted to take pictures with us because, as African-Americans, we were a novelty to them.

We took our children to Senegal at ages when they could appreciate the country, and the experience. During a bus tour to a local university, one young man came up to us, offering ten cows in exchange for our older daughter. She was just twelve years old.

A professor who was accompanying us suggested that the price be raised. It was a joke. He was trying to make light of the situation.

The offer was then upped to one hundred cows. The young gentlemen understood that the girl's parents - us - were both doctors; we would be expecting more.

The young man left after signaling that he would be back. Before we took off, he returned from his meeting with his village fathers, indicating that they had found a way to meet the one hundred cow price.

By this time, our daughter was in tears. It was no longer a joke. Our daughter was priceless, certainly worth more than one hundred cows. It was time to leave.

BIGGER STAGE, HOTTER SUN - ALABAMA

It was 2002. There were many changes in Pittsburgh. There was a desire to have 'more aggressive surgeons', and perhaps those with a different approach to the competitive nature of solid organ transplantation.

In February of 2002, Dr. Courbet died at home. He was a colleague, a phenomenal surgeon, and Director of the Pancreatic Transplant program at University of Pittsburgh.

I was on duty the previous weekend and had completed a transplant early on that Monday morning. It was about 8 AM, and I was on my way home to take a shower, before returning to work. A call came from the operating room asking me if I knew where Dr. Courbet was at that time. I did not know. The call, and the question, sparked feelings of uncertainty and dread.

He did not show up for his case. That was unusual for him. I covered the service for him. This was very unusual.

In an instant, I turned the car toward his home and pulled into the driveway. The front door was open. The screen door was closed. Snow was on the ground outside. There were no tracks in the snow. I rang the doorbell. There was no answer.

Steam was coming from the vent on the side of the condominium. Perhaps someone was home using the dryer. I went to the back porch. The back door was wide open. Snow had blown into the kitchen. I was nervous.

I went to my car and called 911. The police arrived, questioned who I was and what was I doing there. They requested my identification but, this time, I was not directly accused of any wrong-doing.

Police: "Did you enter the house?"

Me: "No I did not."

Police: "Why did you call police?"

Me: "He is a surgeon I work with, and he did not show up at work this morning to operate."

Dr. Courbet was found, dead, in his bedroom. It was later discovered he had been in a motor vehicle accident prior to his death and did not seek medical help. He likely died of a head injury sustained in the accident.

I never understood the significance of both the front and back doors of his home being open when I arrived.

The memory of him lingers. I will be ever grateful for his teachings on pancreatic transplantation, and his unique operative tricks. Who would think that a piece of rubber glove placed up against a leaking arterial anastomosis would reduce the leaking without the need for additional sutures?

It was all in the physics of positive and negative ions, he stated. "Look it up.", he would say.

Concurrently, there was new administrative leadership in the transplantation division, and it was announced that it would be moved in a new, more aggressive, direction.

Coupled with this uncertainty, my husband had also interviewed for a position at University of New Orleans. For me, this would be a new adventure. I had no experience with, or knowledge about, southern lifestyles; only that my husband was the quintessential Southern gentleman. I began my quest for interviews and employment in the region.

There were several opportunities, and yet the most attractive was one where I could make a difference in a region that was very much underserved, while I grew in my career.

Harvey ultimately decided to stay at the University of Pittsburgh, but we agreed that I should be open to other opportunities if they became available.

Meanwhile, those I mentored, and trained, were building programs also. One of our trainees was Dr. Ferdinand Ukah, who completed his fellowship at University of Pittsburgh in 1992, and then went on to University of Iowa and then Alabama. There, he started the kidney transplant program.

Within months of the start of the program, Dr. Ukah set out from Alabama to his homeland of Nigeria. He was going to start his ailing father on the dialysis process.

As he was being driven to the airport, for his flight back to Alabama, he and his car were attacked and he was murdered.

Dr. Ferdinand Ukah left behind, in Alabama, a wife and four young children.

His program, at University of South Alabama, was taken over by another surgeon; he left abruptly.

I respected his work, and what had already been built. This was an opportunity to continue to offer the residents of this southern state with chances for life-changing kidney transplantations. I was ready.

Later that year, I accepted the position in Mobile Alabama, at the University of South Alabama, as Chief of Transplantation and Assistant Dean of Community Outreach and Education.

The deep south did not welcome me with open arms. It was remarked that it was audacious of me to come to my interview with my hair braided. Perhaps it was shocking, but it was not an obstacle.

As one of the many transplant programs governed, and under oversight of the Center for Medicaid and Medicare Services, patients and participants were made aware that, until a new surgeon was added to the staff and team, there would be no transplants. I was called back for a second interview.

On my second interview, all went well with the hospital and university officials whom I met. Lunch with the staff members was light-hearted and warm.

After the official visits were over, I was met at the hotel by a member of the nephrology team serving the area. He proceeded to show me some articles published by the local newspaper. The articles covered several complaints by some of the patients in the region regarding the lack of fair treatment. While mentioning that these complaints were unfounded, the reason for the visit was to let me know that his group would not be referring any patients to me. Instead, they would continue to support the well-established program located four hours away.

The point was made. I was not welcomed.

Once hired, I met again with one of the leading nephrologists who proceeded to question my knowledge on different patient scenarios, conditions, and my proposed methods of treatment. It was likely that he had some patients with troubling medical problems and needed answers on what to do. It was as if I was being deposed to gain in-depth information on kidney patients with hepatitis C.

Despite the lack of direct referrals, or the banning of information disbursal on our transplant program from the dialysis units, the residents knew I was there, and they came as self-referrals.

The initial plan was to hire two surgeons. However, the hiring of the second potential surgeon was cancelled when some previously undisclosed information was brought forth. There was still a plan put forth to hire a second surgeon, each year I was there. This never happened.

After raising my concern about this, I was reminded on several occasions that I was not entirely welcomed:

"Remember, you are not one of us."

"Don't come down here trying to turn this place into a mini-Pittsburgh." "Here in the south, we do things differently."

"You Yankees come here to the south thinking you know everything, and we know nothing."

"We don't do those kinds of things down here."

All the while I thought, "What kind of things? Saving lives? That's all I am about."

Our clinical team consisted of me, a transplant nephrologist and a nurse practitioner. Eventually, our program was acknowledged and embraced by local communities and leaders, both politically and professionally.

Despite the lack of nephrology referrals, patients came because of word-of-mouth and patient testimonials. For many patients, getting to the center, four hours away by car, was impossible. It was our center, or nothing. Many patients who had been listed for over five years at the other center got their needed kidney transplants with us, in Mobile.

The staff was empowered, loved what they did, and participated in educations and outreach eagerly. Patients signed on to educate others on dialysis about the need for transplantation. We continued to thrive, with the help of the Alabama Kidney Fund and the National Kidney Foundation.

We survived and thrived to celebrate our 100th kidney transplant and our ten years as a transplant center; everyone, and especially our patients, was invited to the wonderful gala.

Patients were empowered to become their own advocates. We drew referrals from the Panhandle of Florida, Pensacola to Panama City. As the only transplant surgeon, my travel radius was limited to a one-hour drive from the hospital.

There was a promise to hire a second surgeon from my very first day on the job. It never happened. For the six years of my tenure in Mobile I took calls every night.

Fortunately, once the transplant coordinators were added, the load was lightened considerably. With them taking some of the 'first' calls, I was allowed some nights of sleep. They also took the leadership on outreach to various regions, along with connections with some of the patients.

During one of those occasions, we were canvassing a health fair at a nearby church. An elderly male was asked if he was an organ donor. His response was, "We just got our new organ at our church. I already gave what I could. Sorry Missy."

There was no racial tension with any of the patients or their families. In fact, I often sensed the pride that they had in having me as a surgeon. The general hospital staff also showered me with love and affection, stopping by my office to see if there was anything they could do for me.

There was another side. Some of the patients cared for by the local nephrologists met with objections to being listed for kidney transplantation.

One partially blind, diabetic African-American woman was called in for a transplant. Her nephrologist called to asked why we were treating her with a transplant. According to him, she "was not a benefit to our society."

I explained that I was not in a place to pass judgement on the life of a person, but since she met the criteria for listing, she would be getting a transplant. And so she did, without any complications.

Her abusive husband's first question after coming out of surgery: "Doc, how long do you expect her to live?"

Well, this lady did well, became more independent, and more involved with her church activities. One year later, she even traveled to Detroit to live with her daughter. On her last visit to clinic, dressed sharply, with a bounce in her walk, she announced, "I now, finally have the courage to pack up and leave that ass of a husband of mine. Good riddance! Thank you doctor." Hers was a life well lived and a life well worth it.

On another occasion, there was a 70 year old, robust white male who, in the course of his workup for transplant, was found to have prostate cancer. I referred him to a urologist to be treated for his cancer. A later phone call from the local nephrologist was to let me know that "down here, we don't treat those kinds of cancers!" It was not my practice before and not my area of expertise. Based on his degree of cancer load and age, the course of action recommended showed a definite difference between doctors and cultures in the US North versus South.

The patient was referred for treatment, opted to receive it and later was transplanted, once cleared of his cancer.

The light notes were there too. There was one case where the daughter of a recipient slated for a transplant wanted to know how long her mother's procedure would take. I explained that it would be 3-4 hours before she woke up in the recovery room, including anesthesia time and placing the necessary lines and catheters. The daughter replied, "Why does it take you so long? I've watched a kidney transplant procedure on TV and it only took an hour!" I could not help telling her, "Most shows are only an hour on TV. This is real life, with no commercials!"

RECOGNITION

As Professor of Surgery and Chief of Transplantation, I was recognized for my leadership in many ways. The New Jersey Organ and Tissue Sharing Network recognized the growing number of African-American Transplant Surgeons and sought an opportunity to showcase our accomplishments in an educational outreach day of programming to be followed by a black-tie dinner.

This is the one opportunity that brought together nearly all the African-American Transplant surgeons in this country. Each of us was awarded the Samuel Kountz Heritage Award for 'Forging the Way: Black Transplant Surgeons-Heritage, Hope and Healing'. Along with myself, as the only female surgeon present, were sixteen African-American male transplant surgeons. Among them were: Clive Callender, Clarence Foster, Dale Distant, Cass Franklin. Charles Modlin, Carlton Young, Henry Randall, Okay Odocha, Lynt Johnson, and Devon John as well as Adrian Cotterell, Dorian Wilson and Bob Higgins.

Since that historic event at least twelve new African-American transplant surgeons have joined our ranks.

Ebony Magazine did a feature in its March 2006 edition. I was so excited to see myself in print - clad in green scrubs, in and out of the operating room. It was a story about women, and the many aspects of womanhood. It highlighted our contributions as professionals, corporate leaders, teachers, and the many who fail to get the recognition they deserve. While the cover of the magazine featured LaTanya Richardson and her husband Samuel Jackson, my section covered several pages.

My story was in a national magazine: in newsstands, on coffee tables, in beauty salons and barber shops and if not bought was likely scanned by those who flip pages in line at the supermarkets.

The magazine was also given out in prisons. Perhaps it was traded for a cigarette or some soap. However obtained, I suddenly was inundated with numerous letters from inmates across the country. Listed in the magazine was my location at the University of South Alabama. There came marriage proposals, requests for business entrepreneurships, and even just 'I am so in love' letters. There were many promises to 'look me up' when they were finally residing outside the walls. I did not hold any of them to such promises.

Privileged to be a source of inspiration, I sought opportunities to embrace my community and those in the surrounding regions. Our patients became more committed to the need for greater organ donor education. As a member of the Mobile Chapter of the Links, Incorporated, I spearheaded our 'Linkages to Life' national program. This program focused on Organ Tissue and Bone Marrow Donation awareness. Initiated by the Southern Area chapters, there was a greater need for educating the larger numbers of African-Americans on dialysis, who were not being referred for kidney transplantation in the southern region. With great success, we worked with neighboring churches to attempt to dispel the myths of organ donation, while simultaneously empowering residents to be advocates for their own health.

Previously inducted into the Delta Sigma Theta Sorority as an Honorary member, I was officially recognized by the cities of Mobile and Prichard with my own proclamations, which came from each Mayor's office. There was even a day named after me: Velma Scantlebury Day: March 18th, 2007, by a Resolution from the City Council of Mobile, Alabama.

There were restrictions on my travel, and keeping within a one-hour drive of the hospital, disallowed some of my favorite things. I could not attend conferences or visit family without putting the program on hold. It meant that the patients listed for transplant would have to be notified that no transplant surgeries would be available during my absence.

In 2006 I had the extreme pleasure of being selected as an honorary member of the Delta Sigma Theta Sorority, Incorporated. I as nominated by the late Dr. Yvonne Kennedy, a state representative from Mobile, Alabama, and a former president of Bishop State Community College. She also served as the national president of Delta Sigma Theta sorority from 1988 to 1992.

I was shocked and overwhelmed by the nomination and the selection. Lacking knowledge or opportunity related to sororities during my college years, I welcomed the invitation to be part of the sisterhood of educated women, dedicated to public services and programs within the African-American community. Having accepted the invitation to be inducted at the 48th National Convention in Philadelphia, I had to arrange coverage for our patients while I would be out of town.

Not knowing what to expect and focusing on getting right back to town, I planned to be in Philadelphia for the distinguished induction ceremony for only one day. I flew up the night before, and was escorted the following morning to the Philadelphia Convention Center where the event was taking place.

I recall standing outside the door, with my escorts for what seemed to be an eternity, especially in high heels. Well, finally the doors opened and I entered the convention center to an arena filled with sea of mocha-colored women of all hues. Over ten thousand women, all dressed in white attire. I was wearing a robe, and had to walk a red carpet, all the way to the front.

I was in shock. I was not prepared. The applause never ended, the smiles were everywhere, the greetings were phenomenal. I looked up to see my image on the large screens above, as I had to keep smiling, greeting and containing my surprise and nervousness. This was an experience of a lifetime. I was the only honoree brought into this sisterhood in 2006.

As I the reached to stage, there were others, previously inducted, honorary members seated, and I sat in the open seat, next to Sheryl Lee Ralph. I could not tell you who sat in the other seats. There were thousands of Black women, welcoming me into their sisterhood.

Seeing myself on the big overhead screens made me realize I could not pick my nose or make any funny faces, as 'all eyes were on me.'

After the official pledge and induction ceremony, there were the greetings and pictures; who knows how many hundreds of pictures! I was excited to be part of such a great sorority. Unfortunately, not knowing the particulars or schedule of events of the National Convention, the expected lunches and dinners after the induction ceremony, I apologetically left to return to Mobile. I was nervous being away, despite the fun of having the "paparazzi" following me on my way out. It was a great honor to be there.

DIFFICULT DECISIONS

During my time away, a severely ill patient needed an urgent operation, and was managed by one of the general surgeons. Despite doing all that was surgically possible, the patient expired.

The guilt that flooded me after this occurred, made it clear that I could no longer continue to work alone. Coupled with the guilt of abandoning the residents of the area, I was struggling with the awful decision that needed to be made.

At the same time, three of our young patients developed recurring problems with their kidney transplants; the new kidneys showed signs of their initial illness of the old kidneys attacking the new kidneys again. Thus, the transplanted kidneys became so diseased that they, too, failed in helping those patients to live without the need of dialysis. There was little to be done, as the transplant medications failed to prevent the old disease from attacking the new kidneys. All three patients were young, under the age of thirty.

We were required to track transplant outcomes. Those that failed resulted in a decline in our positive outcomes; we had to be more diligent monitoring in each aspect of our patient selection process. We had to be able to predict which patients would do poorly.

Hospital leadership seized on this fall in our expected outcomes and questioned the legitimacy of the program, and even if it could continue to survive. Those questions dovetailed with new guidelines being put in place by the Center for Medicaid and Medicare Services (CMS).

In 2006, CMS established new guidelines for transplantation that included a new rule that there could no longer be a 'single surgeon' transplant center. The surgeon performing the living donor kidney procedure could not be the same surgeon transplanting the donated kidney into the intended recipient for that kidney.

Also, a transplant surgeon could not take center calls 365 days a year. That was me. Decisions had to be made. Hire another surgeon or close the transplant center.

I was asked to produce a SWOT analysis of the program - Strengths, Weaknesses, Opportunities, and Threats. Patients already scheduled for living donor surgeries were served, with the able aid of a urologic surgeon who was willing to travel from Birmingham, Alabama.

The executive, governing branch of the Medical Center made clear the desire to close the transplant center. Patients protested, wrote letters, held demonstrations, but eventually the battle was lost as the University set its sights on starting a college football team, the South Alabama Jaguars. It was difficult to reconcile the choice; and, it remains so.

THE MOBILE TRANSITION

Mother developed dementia. Thinking back to her first visit to Mobile Alabama, she could not find the bedroom each time she went into the kitchen. She blamed it on the house being too big. It was a ranch house, a simple 4 bedrooms - but not a two- peak Chattel home in Bridgetown Barbados.

I was in Mobile. Alabama had been good, and had been harrowing.

By 2007, mum was getting worse; she did not understand the pain she was experiencing from her severe rheumatoid arthritis. She could not participate in physical therapy because she forgot the instructions.

I wanted, and needed, to contribute to my village, my family. Towards the end of 2006, and with four years of being on call every day and night, I realized that the promises made to add a second surgeon would not be fulfilled. If that did not happen, I would not be able to support my village.

I asked God to show me what to do. It was not in me to abandon my patients in the region. It was not in me to abandon my mother, my hero, my 'first phenomenal woman'. Dad was yearning for my presence but voiced understanding. I was committed to my work.

There were many patients in need of transplants, but with options that could be considered. As we reached out beyond Mobile to the neighboring transplant programs, all of them had to be closer to Mobile than Birmingham, four hours away.

Strictly applied, this would be the rule for my contact with mum. My alternatives had to be closer to home.

The rules had changed. I would no longer be subjected to every night call. It was a mandate. The local patients had to be relocated, and those already transplanted would continue to be under the care of the transplant nephrologist. He would remain in the region.

All of the phone calls were scheduled and completed for the local patients, whose care would continue locally. For the staff, they would be reassigned to various locations throughout the hospital. Some sought employment at other institutions.

The six years of constantly being available for both donor and recipient cases, resulted in my body experiencing chronic fatigue. My brain lost some of its sharpness, and my body longed for a much needed vacation away from it all.

The work had to, and did, go on. We, the entire team, are grateful for the clinical assistance of our nephrologist and the nurse practitioner that participated in the care of our patients. I had patients across the south. I had an ailing mother in New York City.

Traveling from Mobile Alabama to New York always meant making a connecting flight. It also meant that there was nearly no opportunity to get there before noon without coming in the night before. With sick parents, the stress of not being able to be there at crucial times was destroying me. Overall, I knew it was time to leave Alabama.

God provided me with a way to get closer to my parents without failing our patients.

The University of Mississippi, only 2 hours away, was willing to create a satellite office for those who would be transferred to their center; but, all would be managed in Mobile by one of our own transplant coordinators, hired by University of Mississippi.

This would allow the patients to be transplanted more quickly, as Mississippi had a larger number of donors and a smaller waiting list.

While patients were not happy, the reality was there was no choice; and the visiting team from Mississippi was fabulous at reassuring them about the continuity and quality of the services offered.

The closing of the Mobile program provided me with the opportunity to move closer to my parents and family. My husband would not need to commute as far, as he still held his position as Associate Professor at University of Pittsburgh. The girls hated to move again, understandably so, since they were within one and two years of graduating from high school. But as children usually do, they adjusted. The deal breaker was no more required school uniforms: it would be public schools.

Within weeks of moving back north, my mother took ill and had to be hospitalized. It was a blessing to be close and able to reach New York in a matter of hours.

I was certain that God had created a path for me to better survive, both mentally and physically. It also gave me a sense of relief to be there for my aging parents at a time when they needed me the most.

And indeed they did. From progressive dementia, to worsening arthritis and immobility from joint swelling, my 'phenomenal woman' would occasionally recognize me only as 'her last child': no name. That was good enough. Somewhere inside, the wicked disease took her joy away and slowly she was there no more. She was present in body, already absent in mind. There was sadness, but less pain. Eventually, she was pain-free; she ceased to exist physically. She had given of herself, for her family, for me to get beyond that yellow wall.

God is good; all the time.

SACHIN - MATTERS

Dr. Starzl had a special place in his heart for children. Perhaps the memory of the first human liver transplant he performed in 1963 at the University of Colorado would be the force he needed to move beyond conventional thinking. While this 3 year-old child died on the operating table, his unrelenting desire to better understand the bleeding and rejection seen after many unsuccessful liver transplants, drove him to seek answers. It would be 1967 before he would achieve success in human liver transplantation.

And so, when others saw hopelessness, he saw opportunities. He could not turn his back on a young American child abroad with a ruptured, cancerous liver. While others were reluctant, he never hesitated to offer her help.

She was flown from a US Navy base in Hong Kong to Children's Hospital of Pittsburgh.

Sachin had taken ill while shopping with her parents in Hong Kong. She was found to have had a ruptured hepatoblastoma, which was explored by other surgeons. It was thought to be hopeless.

Dr. Starzl performed a liver transplant on this young recipient despite much objection from the transplant community. We watched as he washed out the abdomen with several liters of saline to rid it of any cancer cells. He did what was thought to be impossible.

Once recovered from surgery, Sachin would receive six months of chemotherapy as part of her cancer treatment. But the side effects of the drugs caused her much discomfort, sadness, and overall malaise. Her parents questioned the value of the treatment versus the quality of the life she had during the treatment.

They returned home to the Philippines, so that Sachin could live a more normal life, like any regular three-year-old. There was nothing regular about Sachin. She had her own personal attendant, her own doctor, nurse and general staff. I never recall seeing her walk while she was in Pittsburgh, as her feet hardly ever touch the ground.

Twelve years later Sachin and her parents returned to Pittsburgh from the Philippines along with her personal staff to request use of growth hormone to allow her to get taller.

Sachin was 4 feet 10 1/2 inches but wanted to be 5 feet so that she could one day be president of the Philippines. The rationale was that there was a requirement (according to Sachin) that any president would have to be at least 5 feet tall.

During this visit it was discovered that her immunosuppressive therapy had been sub therapeutic over the last twelve years since leaving Pittsburgh. Due to a minor misunderstanding by her doctors, her drug levels were drawn after she took the dose of the drugs rather than before.

Since Sachin had taken very little medication over the previous years, she was weaned off all medication before her return to the Philippines. Dr. Starzl was at the time in the midst of a trial of weaning (tapering off) the anti-rejection medications of many transplanted patients. He saw Sachin as a great candidate. After a biopsy to confirm that there was no rejection in her liver transplant, he stopped all her medications.

Sachin remained cancer free and rejection free.

Sachin did well long-term without any drugs. Ten years later at the age of 26, she married the love of her life. Her father walked her down the aisle to give her away in matrimony. No one could have predicted her long-term success. However, Dr. Starzl took a chance on this beautiful young toddler and won. That's what he was all about: unconventional practices to save lives.

RHONDA - MATTERED

Over the years as a transplant surgeon, there were persons who entered my life as patients and stayed connected as close and dear friends. Rhonda was one of them. It was her journey as a kidney transplant recipient that caused me to understand not just the medical issues but the social and emotional tolls on patients. As physicians, we can often have our 'heads in the sand' when it comes to such matters. This is how I met Rhonda.

Dr. Mark Hardy ran a relatively drama-free operating room. As a resident we rotated through the Columbia University transplant program to gain 'hands-on', operational transplant experience, I had the opportunity to learn from him. I also had the opportunity to share in how a transplant surgeon's skills touch lives.

For weeks before her operation I had gotten to know Rhonda, a grant writer. She was a woman devoted to finding ways to open up opportunities for others. She had contracted Hepatitis C with her first kidney transplant, and was now in need of a second one.

The day before I had visited Rhonda, along with Dr. Hardy, and it was as if she was giving us assurances. Her unbounded sense of hope was completely intact, and openly shared.

The teams entered the operating room where, as I looked around, the masks and gowns made us all disappear into only the roles we would play in saving Rhonda's life. My place was at Dr. Hardy's side.

His hands worked deliberately and he only spoke to explain things he knew I did not already know. The anesthesiologist chose soothing music, played by a string quartet; it was a wonderful softness in the background of the hard, cold, clean surfaces of the operating room. Again, the bluish light left no plane or corner warm or dark.

The second kidney transplant for Rhonda was a success at every level. Rhonda responded well to everything. The team worked through a smooth set of events and watched a master teacher help a resident improve and gain even more confidence.

It was my job to close the skin layers at the end of the procedures.

Unbeknownst to me, that portion of my contribution would become a conversation starter. Rhonda was thrilled with the delicacy of my closing incision; and, she would remind me of how proud I should have been of my skills. She was proud of that scar as a symbol of one more triumph she made over the odds. She had her own walls; and, she scaled them with our help.

Rhonda made it a point to stay in touch with me as my career progressed. She also would talk about her life, and what it was like to have a failing kidney, the issues with memory recall and the difficulties with knowing what she was supposed to be doing each day. Now with a new kidney, she was back on track. She became more involved in the quest for organ donors and sought ways to stay involved.

I welcomed that contact and saw the relationship as a turning point in how a doctor can touch a life, not just a body.

When my career took me to Pittsburgh, Rhonda would contact me not just about the state of her health, but she wanted to share details about her life. She wanted me to be successful and happy also. After moving to New Jersey, she became involved with nearby transplant centers, and worked with several colleagues who also trained in Pittsburgh. She embraced her ability to be of help to others.

Rhonda's body betrayed her again, years later. She needed a third kidney transplant. Following that successful journey, Rhonda gave me all the details about the third operation and the team that cared for her. She was still most complimentary about my previous incision, compared to her more recent one

The relationship had gone on for nearly thirty years. Rhonda even attended my wedding.

Her life had come to include a young Black girl. She called upon me to give her advice about how to care for a Black girl's hair. Late one night I received a call with the sound of desperation.

"Heh Velma, what is hair grease? Belle said I should grease her scalp like her mother does it. What is grease?"

We both laughed for the next ten minutes, after enlightening her on issues with Black hair.

It was a far cry from my other role as advisor on her medical challenges.

After she moved to Charlotte North Carolina, we were able to connect on a few occasions when a meeting took me in that direction. As the years passed, she developed issues with heart disease and multiple other medical problems.

True to her unwavering, upbeat nature when Rhonda went into hospice, she sought to shield me from the news. She felt that I had given so much, I should not have to worry about her; this was especially true since we were no longer near one another. She gave her doctor instructions to wait until after her demise to call and inform me.

Her life, and eventual death, were illustrative of how a woman could, and should, lead a proud and independent life. Her physical struggles were masked, or overcome, by her indomitable positive spirit. Her status in our health care system was more difficult to fathom and conquer.

The Medicare system has limits, and eventually stops working for any person who is in the aftermath of a transplant procedure. The rules state that when a patient has survived for three years following the procedures there will be no further support from the Medicare system. This was the case with Rhonda.

Rhonda's transplants were more than three years apart, and the system placed her back at square one each time she survived.

Rhonda's boundless hope, and the positive energy she injected into our relationship touched my life. What happened, since my part in Rhonda's second transplant was a template for the way the lives of transplant surgeons and patients can intertwine.

Eventually, there was little more that could be done for Rhonda, and the woman I had come to think of more as a long-distance friend than just a former patient died. Her physical heart failed, not her spirit.

FRIEDA - MATTERED

When the patient is your exact age and they are so close to death that you can smell the bad odor, it can propel you into an avalanche of remedies to restore hope in the system. She was not allowed to die. She was a young mother of three with a doting husband who were all reassured that bringing her to Pittsburgh meant she would be awake again, once her new liver was in place.

Frieda was from Memphis and her own doctors felt this was where she needed to be.

She presented with acute Hepatitis B, and had gone into a coma. Neither she nor her husband knew she was so devastatingly ill or near death.

Her children hugged her and watched with tearful eyes as we wheeled her into the operating suite. A new liver was on its way. Prayers went up for her.

Her body's failure was acute. The bad liver has caused a build-up of toxins in her brain. It resulted in poor brain function. It was reversible, but we had to work fast.

Time, success, and experience allowed me to take the role of team leader for the procedures Frieda needed.

The first hour was routine. It did not belie what lay ahead.

Near hour three, the room became pin-drop silent. There was no banter to pass between teams or team-mates. Just the noise of the constant suctioning of blood lost with dissection of her tissues. There were small and larger blood vessels everyplace we explored.

Over the next four hours, team members rotated in, and out, of the operating theatre, offering higher levels of skill to achieve our purpose.

The day ground on. Parts of me hurt. I was tired. Yet, as team leader, I could not stop; I could not lose focus.

I could feel droplets of sweat trying to escape my scrubs, as well as a numbness in my hip. My eyes felt as though they would never work anywhere other than peering over my mask and into the blue-white, hot light illuminating Frieda.

There is always blood in transplant procedures; lots of it. Frieda was a special case. The liver produces enzymes that aid in making blood clot. For Frieda, this was no longer the case.

As we entered the sixth hour of work, we had used over fifty units of blood to keep her systems alive.

The clusters of veins, clustered around the kidney, and lying beneath and above Frieda's liver were varicosed. They were everywhere.

The only time I could remember throwing my head back, looking away, was in deciding to save the kidney, which was removed in order to better access the bleeding below the liver. As I looked up from the open body, I was asking for help and guidance from above.

I could not do it alone. I still needed other team members for support as we were tired and still had a challenge ahead of us.

I had a patient who believed in me. The small rush of air that cooled my eyes as I looked up was refreshing. It was also something I took as a sign.

The next best way to control the bleeding was to remove the right kidney with all the attached blood vessels. It had to be done to move to the next step.

I instructed the team to place the removed kidney in a pan, to save it for the next steps. All the years of watching and learning had my brain give new instructions to my hands.

It was time to remove the failed liver, finally to be replaced by the new one. The old kidney was, eventually, placed back in her pelvis by Dr. Shapiro, once the patient was stabilized.

Frieda survived. Our team walked, with the slow and halting steps of men and women whose knees have been locked for hours. On the floor were the old blood soaked blankets used at our feet to absorb what leaked under the drapes that separated her from us. As we shuffled out, knowing that the liver was better and that Frieda's body accepted her old kidney again, shoulders dropped and breathing became deeper again. Relief was never so welcomed.

Each of Frieda's birthdays was marked with a call she made to thank me for its existence. Each of my birthdays was marked with a call she made to express her happiness that I had come into her life. She often would call when she saw a new doctor. She had to explain that her kidney transplant was her own kidney.

"Tell me again how that came to be so. I forgot what you told me the last time."

I was at the edge of watching her children become adults, and I came to know the grandchildren, by names and verbal descriptions. She enjoyed her family, even as it grew.

Frieda and I remained in touch, until her death twenty years later. Her liver did well, but, she later developed renal failure from the anti-rejection medications.

Her liver also developed scarring from recurrent Hepatitis B. She was started on peritoneal dialysis to cleanse her system of the toxins her kidney could no longer remove. Frieda applied to be listed for a kidney transplant.

Unfortunately, she was rejected due to liver disease and was recommended for a combined liver and kidney transplant. She remained on dialysis for nearly 8 years with stable liver function. Despite her diseased condition, it was not severe enough to get a new liver, but scarred enough to prevent her from getting a kidney alone.

Frieda moved back to Nashville, and never failed to seek advice about her medical management and concerns. Her final infection resulted in a prolonged hospitalization and she reached out to me, asking me to take her as my patient. I was no longer in Pittsburgh, and lacked the ability to provide her with better options of care.

Her earnest pleas for help, and her entreaties to be allowed to leave the hospital, continue to haunt me. I was not in a position to transfer her. I felt helpless.

Eventually, her infection led to worsening liver disease and she passed away without getting re-transplanted.

I still miss those cards and the continuing conversation. Her calls would always start with, "Hi Doc, what are you doing? This is Frieda".

Everyone should experience touching another's life so deeply. As a surgeon, as a mentor, one can touch another life just as intimately.

RETURN TO THE VILLAGE - BUILD A VILLAGE

I love mentoring.

Dr. Joycelyn Elders, past Surgeon General of the United States, told us all, "You can't be what you can't see."

I truly believe this. I married a man who had many 'children'; students he mentored from the time he was in a position to do so.

Being mentored helped me. It helped my husband's students. I become a mentor instantly. Whether at middle or high schools, churches or community gatherings, I am always profoundly humbled by the numerous letters received from young students whose lives were impacted by my story.

I gave them hope when there was fear. They saw possibilities instead of barriers; instead of walls.

I now can look back on that large pile of correspondence and only hope that they were able to get beyond their own walls to pursue their dreams. From Dana to Edith and Mi Lee to Javon, Emilia, Madison, Amira, Isaac and Danielle, know that your success is my success.

More needed to be done, and still needs to be done.

As a junior attending, my chairman handed me a credit card so that I could meet with the female surgical residents for dinner on a bi-annual basis. He saw a need for the interactions, and facilitating them.

Whether it was junior fellows in transplantation, or medical students interested in surgery, there was always room in our home, especially for Sunday dinner.

Our girls grew up knowing that our home would have student guests with each holiday or Sunday meal.

Nora was one of those guests. As a college student, she came to me initially for a summer internship. An operating room nurse, who was aware that Nora wanted to be a doctor, immediately thought of me as a mentor, leader, and role-model.

Born in South Sudan, her family self-exiled to South Africa for political reasons. She emigrated to the United States at age sixteen to attend New Rochelle College. At the end of her first year, Nora needed a place to stay for the summer while school was closed. The hope was that I would provide her with a place to stay and she could shadow me for the summer.

Nora stayed with us that summer, and for each holiday after that. She remained interested in medicine and was able to gain from the shadowing experiences I provided during her college years.

With our help she was able to apply to various schools and was accepted into Georgetown University. I could not persuade her to do surgery, but she developed an interest in anesthesiology. As one of her 'American' parents, Harvey had the honor of walking her down the aisle when she was married. She and her husband are now the proud parents of 3 loving children. They call us their grandparents. Nora currently practices in San Antonio, Texas.

ADENIKE

When I met her, she was in college. I had been invited to speak to aspiring students interested in medicine at a nearby college for women.

After the conference, Adenike came up and boldly introduced herself and voiced her interest in being a doctor. I became her mentor.

Our relationship blossomed during her years in college. Born in Nigeria, she was alone in Pittsburgh, but could be found at our home for Sunday and Holiday dinners. Our relationship extended beyond the common interest of medicine, as she would often babysit for our girls. She also had wonderful skills in hair braiding.

After college, graduating with a degree in chemistry, she accepted a position with an insurance company. While she enjoyed her job, I knew she had a greater purpose in life. Encouraging her to apply for a position in one of our laboratories, she was immediately interviewed by the supervisor, and was hired.

Despite being the only African-American in the lab at that time, she was not discouraged. Years later, Adenike shared with me the significance of my call to her that day.

She had become complacent, enjoying her job at the insurance company. She had almost forgotten her dream of becoming a physician.

She became re-focused, and surrounded by an atmosphere of encouragement.

Adenike has an incredibly contagious laugh. She knew what she wanted out of life and was not going to let anything get in her way. I had the pleasure of working with her on several clinical projects, where she collected patient data for analysis.

Adenike was rejected from medical school on her first two attempts. Knowing that she needed to do something different to boost her credentials while she worked full time, she took higher level courses and received all A's. She improved her MCAT scores and applied to medical school for a third time.

Adenike was persistent in checking in with the admissions office to verify if all her information was received. She called to see if she would be granted an interview. She called to see when she would be interviewed.

We set out to make sure that any walls we encountered, any sink-holes encountered would not be surprises for her. We succeeded.

After being rejected twice before, Thomas Jefferson Medical College added her to the wait-list and the next year admitted her without an interview.

Her persistence, in calling the admissions office to check on the process of her application, certainly played a significant role in her being offered a conditional acceptance.

She showed her sincere commitment to becoming a doctor.

She was smart, determined, and willing to overcome any obstacles that were in her way.

Adenike knew 'walls'. She, too, had learned to beat back the intimidation.

Her actions and experience are reminiscent of the story of a young man who went for a job and was turned down. Every day he went back to the office to ask for the job and was turned away every day.

He returned, yet other days, expecting the same answer. One of those days, the boss was so frustrated seeing him come there every day that he finally gave him a job.

I think of Adenike every time I think of this story. Adenike did not want to be overlooked. She checked to make sure nothing was missing from her application. Her persistence paid off. She completed medical school, residency and practiced in Minneapolis for many years. She makes me very proud of her success. She is currently practicing in Maryland, and is married with 3 sons.

Each one of us that has learned, should teach others how to breach the walls placed before them. It can be considered, by some as an option - but by me - as an obligation!

KATE

Kate knew she was going to be a pediatric surgeon.

It was God's plan for her to come to Pittsburgh to do a research year in the middle of her general surgery training program in Brooklyn New York.

She worked under the leadership of Dr. Henri Forde at Children's Hospital of Pittsburgh, as an integral part of his research team. Her work led to publications and presentations, and eventually she was accepted into the general surgery residency program at the University of Pittsburgh. That was how we met. There were few other residents of color at the time, and certainly no females.

Kate was a welcomed addition to the department of surgery, even as a resident. She was jovial, smiled constantly, and walked with a bounce. As we were often seen together, many assumed she was my daughter, because we 'looked so much alike'. After constantly explaining that we were not, we just went with the flow. Yes, she was my daughter.

And, she was considered a daughter by our family. I became her mentor, accompanying her to the surgical office to discuss some ridiculous report or evaluation. One attending reported her because 'it was abnormal for a resident to be overly happy all the time'.

Kate excelled.

She completed her pediatric surgery training, and despite many hurdles, is now well established in a practice in Philadelphia. She is the proud mother of three boys.

If Kate mentors five others; if Adenike mentors five others – think.

THE GROUP IS GLORIOUS

"I can do all things through Christ who strengtheneth me." Philippians 4:13

It was my life's dream to be a doctor, initially a pediatrician. Later, I was bitten by the 'surgical bug', as a first-year medical student.

It has been 30 years since the completion of my multi-organ transplantation fellowship at the University of Pittsburgh. I was more than fortunate to earn a position with the Thomas E. Starzl Transplantation Institute.

I saw the success of the good doctor Starzl, and those before him, such as Dr. Kenneth Forde, a Black surgeon. He, like me, was from Barbados.

There is no way to note all those who inspired me over the years. I can, though, help build a legacy. I can mentor, inspire, cajole, promote, pester, and admonish. Most of all, I can support. I can support all those who have to go beyond still existing walls, beyond every wall that will be erected.

There have always been groups aware of, or partially responsible for, my successes. I bow to those groups. I admonish those younger to grow our group of dedicated medical professionals exponentially.

Together: with the help of others, I succeeded. Together: those following can lift one another up. The help of the group is glorious. Use it.

Find a mentor. Use that support. Support another.

FROM THE 'GOOD DOCTOR' BARLOW

The passion of Dr. Barbara Barlow, the first female attending, and head of the division of Pediatric Surgery at Harlem Hospital Center, an affiliate of Columbia University, was a rocket propelling me on my path.

Each person I mentor, can bring in another five. Imagine how many new, 'good doctors', we can generate and help to thrive.

There was, for me, the 'Good Doctor Barlow' There were mentors. There should scores more 'Good Doctors'.

Become one! Use me.

My belief in God, my strength, is in faith. It works; and, is sustaining. So is my faith in the power of each of us teaching, learning from, pulling up, and listening to each other.

I hope my success over the past 30 years inspires others to become more deeply involved with mentoring, and helping the next waves to stand higher against the shore, and overcome the walls built to keep us out.

For the past twenty years I have said that I would not consider retirement until there are ten other transplant women of color. We have surpassed ten, and one of them has already taken the initiative to name our group "Mocha Women in Transplantation Surgery". We come in all shades.

MOCHA WOMEN IN TRANSPLANTATION SURGERY

Perhaps, ten mentees is too low a number. We have walls to conquer and lives to change, and save. My story is just the beginning. It is a hard-won and costly, but achieved, goal. All the battles have been memorable and worthwhile, even if unfair and unnecessary.

Ten 'mocha women', like me, providing support and mentorship in the science and art of transplantation will develop a legion of 'Good Doctors'.

My initial number is low. Perhaps I can, and will, do more. We all can.

I have numerous peers, heroines and icons in my life that deserve recognition. We school one another. We are always available to help each other go beyond walls, beyond the progress any one of us has made in our pursuits.

Many of the young women have I met on this journey, were encountered at our Society of Black Academic Surgeons annual meetings.

All, though, are part of my village of achievers breaking down walls. I am pleased to be in their company.

I would hope that my career journey has helped pave the way for them, and others, to embrace the rigorous, hectic, and wonderful life of being a woman in transplant surgery.

MOCHA WOMEN IN TRANSPLANTATION - RISE !

Dr. RoseMarie Toussaint was the next Black, female fellow trained in Pittsburgh.

She finished her general surgery at Howard University and completed her transplantation Fellowship at the University of Pittsburgh in 1991. Her contribution and belief in what we can accomplish is invaluable.

Dr. Sherilyn Gordon-Burroughs

Dr. Gordon-Burroughs came to the University of Pittsburgh as a research fellow working under Dr. Henri Forde in the Department of Pediatric Surgery. She later went on to complete her Transplantation Fellowship at the University of California at Los Angeles, with a focus on intestinal transplantation. On March 19, 2017, at the young age of 48, she was killed. It was an apparent murder-suicide carried out by her late husband. She left behind a four year old daughter.

No matter our attained stations in life, it is important to understand that every household can be a paradise, a hell, or both.

When domestic violence pervades a home, there is often a stigma attached to identifying it, and speaking aloud about it. Women, in particular, and men, can be domestic violence victims on a regular basis. Often, too often, there is a reticence to speak out. It is my hope that this changes, radically.

No one knew about Sherilyn's home issues. She did not reach out to family and friends.

Sherilyn was an Associate Professor of Surgery at Houston's Methodist Hospital, and the Assistant Dean of Graduate Medical Education. As a pioneer, leader, and dedicated surgeon on the rise, she was cut down too soon.

I pray that she rests in peace.

Dr. Jacentha Buggs

Dr. Buggs became the first African-American to complete the general surgery residency program at the University of South Florida (USF). Later, she became the first transplant fellow to complete the fellowship program at LifeLink Healthcare Institute, now Tampa General Medical Group (TGMG), Tampa General Hospital, and the University of South Florida.

Dr. Buggs is an organ procurement surgeon and the research specialist at TGMG's transplant surgical team. She also oversees TGMG's summer research program with USF.

Dr. Linda Jane Chen

Linda Jane completed her clinical fellowship at Stanford University, and became an Assistant Professor of Surgery at the University of Miami, Miller School of Medicine. She specializes in kidney and pancreas transplantation at the Miami Transplant Institute. Dr. Chen received her medical degree from the University of Wisconsin, and, at this writing, has been in practice for over 23 years.

Dr. Jennifer McGee

Jennifer McGee completed her surgical training at Tulane University School of Medicine. In addition to clinical outcomes research, Dr. McGee also completed fellowship training in transplant and dialysis procedures. She currently practices general surgery in New Orleans, Louisiana, with ongoing interest in transplantation and dialysis procedures.

Christie W. Gooden, M.D., M.P.H.

Dr. Gooden completed her transplantation fellowship at University of Michigan in Ann Arbor in 2011. She completed her residency in general surgery at the University of Alabama at Birmingham Medical Center. Currently, she works as an abdominal transplant surgeon at Medical City Dallas Texas.

Dr. Terra Pearson

Dr. Pearson completed her Transplantation Fellowship in 2016 at the University of Washington Medical Center. Having trained in general surgery in Detroit, as well as completing a critical care fellowship at nearby Wayne State University, she joined the Medical College of Wisconsin in 2016, where her skills and leadership as an Assistant Professor of Surgery, extend to both adult and pediatric Transplantation.

Dr. Arika Hoffman

Dr. Hoffman is an Assistant Professor of Surgery, and specializes in pediatric transplantation at the University of Nebraska Medical Center. She completed her fellowship at University of Birmingham, Alabama, in 2015.

Constance Mobley, M.D., Ph.D.

Constance Mobley finished her fellowship training in Organ Transplantation at University of California Los Angeles in 2013. Previously, she completed her M.D., Ph.D. at Vanderbilt School of Medicine, followed by general surgery and critical care specialty training. In 2014, Constance joining the staff at Methodist Hospital in Houston Texas, specializing in Transplantation as well as Acute and Critical Care Surgery.

Dr. Dinee Simpson

Dinee is currently an Assistant Professor of Surgery (Organ Transplantation) at the Northwestern University, the Feinberg School of Medicine. She joined this institution after completing her Transplant Fellowship at the University of Pennsylvania in 2017.

Dr. Praise Matemavi

As of this writing, Praise is working through her Transplantation Fellowship at the University of Nebraska. We all look forward to her successful completion of the program in 2019.

Our relationship began with correspondence about her interest in transplantation in 2015.

Dr. Praise Matemavi hails from Zimbabwe, and loves to blog. In her blogs, she shares her life experiences, including the trials and triumphs of being a young mother of 2 children, while pursuing a career in medicine. She also shares with others a past home-life fraught with physical and mental abuse.

Praise Matemavi is going beyond walls set before her.

Dr. Lisa McElroy is currently at the University of Michigan, where she will complete her fellowship in Abdominal Transplantation in 2019. Dr. McElroy obtained her Masters in Health Services and Outcomes Research, along with completion of a postdoctoral fellowship, from Northwestern University in 2014 and 2015 respectively. Her other interests include hepatobiliary surgery and dialysis access procedures.

Dr. Keisha Bonner

Keisha trained at the Mayo Clinic in Rochester Minnesota, finishing her transplantation fellowship in 2018. Dr. Bonner is also a product of the general surgery training programs at Harlem Hospital Center, a place where I also trained.

Dr. Iyore James

Iyore was raised in Nigeria, the continent of Africa.

She completed her general surgery residency, followed by an Abdominal Organ Transplantation fellowship, at Ohio State's University Medical Center, in 2016. Dr. James has a strong interest in modernizing and democratizing the practice of surgery, globally.

It is my sincere hope that my struggles, accomplishments, and examples, in the quest of a democratized medical training and practice system, continue to inspire leaders such as Dr. Iyore James.

Her particular interest, bringing new surgical techniques to sub-Sahara Africa, is a passion. Dr. James practices general surgery in Southern Ohio while providing living donor kidney transplantation services in Nigeria.

More, thank you to my village, my villages, and the villages we will create through more mentorship - going beyond every wall.

I CHALLENGE US

I challenge each of us to bring ten, twenty, or more. The walls are high. Our power and strength, as a sisterhood and in camaraderie with brotherhoods, is vital and it is un-sung.

Sing it.

BRAVE, BOLD, BEST - Dr. Starzl

It has been a career with many twists and turns. For that reason, to all who shared, I am forever grateful for the leadership and training, at each step along the way.

My village, my mentor set, is only complete with ample credit being given to a master surgeon who was also a friend.

Thirty-two years ago, I moved to Pittsburgh to begin a Transplantation Fellowship as a means to become more qualified as a pediatric surgeon. Dr. Starzl opened that door, just as he had opened the door to successful liver transplantation two decades earlier.

Dr. Starzl passed away on March 4th, 2017, at the age of 90, seven days before his 91st birthday. Known as the 'Father of Modern Transplantation' he paved the way for hundreds of surgeons to follow his legacy.

I am humbled to have had the opportunity to benefit from his knowledge, his contributions regarding surgical technique. I am privileged to say that he considered me a friend - and then a colleague, his was lofty company.

On the first year of his death, Dr. Starzl was again honored with the unveiling of his statue on the University of Pittsburgh campus. It was a place where he often walked, played with his dogs, and probably commiserated with the muses of surgery on how to move us all forward.

Indeed, it is a fitting tribute. Anyone can now sit next to him and imagine him conversing about whatever was on his mind at the time. Thank you, Dr. Starzl.